	Calories	Per
Marrow (U.S. marrow squash), raw	4	1 oz.
Mushrooms		
raw	2	1 oz.
fried	62	1 oz.
Mustard and cress	3	1 oz.
Onion, raw	7	1 oz.
Parsnip, raw	14	1 oz.
Peas		
fresh or frozen	20	1 oz.
canned	24	1 oz.
Pepper		
green, raw	9	1 oz.
red, raw	10	1 oz.
Potato		
raw, as purchased	25	1 oz.
old, boiled	23	1 oz.
old, chips (U.S. French fries)	68	1 oz.
old, roast	35	1 oz.
new, boiled	21	1 oz.
crisps (U.S. chips)	159	1 oz.
instant (powder)	100	1 oz.
sweet, boiled	23	1 oz.
Radish	4	1 oz.
Spinach, frozen	7	1 oz.
Swede		
raw	6	1 oz.
boiled	5	1 oz.
Sweetcorn, frozen	27	1 oz.
Tomato		
fresh	4	1 oz.
canned	43	8-oz. can
Turnip		
raw	5	1 oz.
boiled	3	1 oz.
Watercress	4	1 oz.

FRUIT

	Calories	Per
Apple		
dessert	13	1 oz.
cooking, peeled and cored	10	1 oz.
cooking, baked	11	1 oz.
cooking, stewed without sugar	9	1 oz.
Apricots		
fresh	8	1 oz.
canned in syrup	30	1 oz.
dried, raw	52	1 oz.
Avocado pear	25	1 oz.
Banana, without skin	22	1 oz.
Blackberries	8	1 oz.
Blackcurrants, raw	8	1 oz.
Cherries, fresh, with stones (U.S. with pits)	11	1 oz.
Currants, dried	69	1 oz.
Damsons, with stones	9	1 oz.
Dates		
with stones	61	1 oz.
without stones	70	1 oz.
Gooseberries, green, raw	5	1 oz.
Grapefruit		
as purchased, fresh	3	1 oz.
canned in syrup	23	1 oz.
Grapes		
black (U.S. purple)	18	1 oz.
green	17	1 oz.

	Calories	Per
Greengages, with stones	13	1 oz.
Lemon		
as purchased	4	1 oz.
juice only	2	1 oz.
Mandarin oranges, canned in syrup	18	1 oz.
Melon, flesh only	7	1 oz.
Orange		
as purchased	8	1 oz.
natural juice	11	1 oz.
Peaches		
fresh, as purchased	9	1 oz.
canned in syrup	25	1 oz.
Pear, dessert	11	1 oz.
Pineapple		
fresh	13	1 oz.
canned in syrup	22	1 oz.
Plums		
fresh, dessert, with stones	10	1 oz.
canned in syrup	22	1 oz.
Prunes, stewed without sugar	19	1 oz.
Raisins	70	1 oz.
Raspberries		
fresh	7	1 oz.
canned in syrup	33	1 oz.
Redcurrants, raw	6	1 oz.
Rhubarb, raw	2	1 oz.
Strawberries, fresh	7	1 oz.
Sultanas (U.S. seedless white raisins)	71	1 oz.
Tangerine, as purchased	7	1 oz.

NUTS

	Calories	Per
Almonds, shelled	170	1 oz.
Chestnuts, shelled	49	1 oz.
Coconut		
flesh only	104	1 oz.
desiccated (U.S. shredded)	178	1 oz.
Peanuts, shelled	171	1 oz.
Walnuts, shelled	156	1 oz.

FATS AND DAIRY PRODUCE

	Calories	Per
Butter	226	1 oz.
Cheese		
Cheddar	120	1 oz.
Cheshire	110	1 oz.
cottage cheese	30	1 oz.
cream cheese (depending on fat content)	140–232	1 oz.
curd	39	1 oz.
Danish Blue	103	1 oz.
Edam	88	1 oz.
Gruyère	132	1 oz.
Parmesan	118	1 oz.
Cream		
single	62	1 oz.
double	131	1 oz.
sour cream	57	1 oz.
Dream topping, whipped	34	1 fl. oz.
Egg		
standard	90	one
fried, one standard	136	one
yolk only	99	1 oz.
white only	11	1 oz.
Lard	262	1 oz.

(Continued on back endpaper)

SLIMMERS' COOKBOOK

Zita Alden

Hamlyn
London · New York · Sydney · Toronto

Acknowledgements

The author and publishers would like to thank the following for their help and cooperation in supplying colour pictures for this book:

Cadbury Schweppes Foods Limited: page 63.
'Carmel' Agrexco (Agricultural Export Company Limited of Israel): page 19.
Dutch Dairy Bureau: pages 27 and 51.
Fruit Producers' Council: page 23.
Hermes Sweeteners Limited (Hermesetas): page 31.
Kellogg Company of Great Britain Limited: page 59.
Lea and Perrins Worcestershire Sauce: page 55.

The author would like to extend especial thanks to Dorothy Parkes for her invaluable help with research into this book.

Consultant Dietitian—Susan Chappell
Illustrations by Gay John Galsworthy

Published by
The Hamlyn Publishing Group Limited
London · New York · Sydney · Toronto
Hamlyn House, Feltham, Middlesex, England
© Copyright The Hamlyn Publishing Group Limited 1973

ISBN 0 600 38036 X

Printed by Cox and Wyman Ltd., Fakenham, England

Contents

Introduction

It is perfectly possible to slim quickly, by just cutting down on all the so-called 'fattening' foods. The popularity of crash diets shows this. However, this weight loss is seldom permanent as no-one can stick to a very restricted diet for long.

Doctors agree that it is far better to start a diet which will eventually alter your eating habits, allowing yourself all foods within reason, but just counting calories and making sure you stick to around 1,000 calories a day. Small weight losses over many weeks produce more permanent results than a spectacular weight loss in the first week of dieting and then nothing much after that.

After the first two or three weeks of slimming, a weight loss of two pounds each week is a realistic goal and one which can be achieved without sacrificing sound nutrition.

Since no single food provides all the nutrients we need in exactly the right quantities, we require a variety of foods each day. Even foods which we know are very nutritious, such as milk and liver, will not supply all the different nutrients we need.

It is much easier to balance your meals if you classify foods, putting all similar foods together and then thinking of the whole group. Then, when working out your menus, choose at least one food from each group.

Protein foods These are the foods usually chosen for your main course and include meats, fish, eggs, cheese, poultry and bacon. Other foods such as sausages and luncheon meats also fall into this category, but they contain less protein, more fat and usually some added starch.

Everyone needs proteins because these foods supply the raw material from which our bodies build new tissues. So important are they that you should aim to include a protein food at each meal during the day. Protein foods are especially important during slimming because you want to keep your lean tissues intact as the fat vanishes.

Much of your daily vitamin and mineral requirements are also obtained from the protein foods, especially those like liver, kidney and corned beef which are rich in iron. Iron is found only in very small quantities in other foods, so the perfectly balanced diet should include one serving of either liver, kidney or corned beef each week.

One of the great advantages of protein foods for the slimmer is that they give a 'full up' feeling and keep you feeling satisfied for longer periods of time than other foods do, so they help you to stop nibbling between meals.

Vegetables Most vegetables are rich in vitamins and minerals and low in calories, so they can be eaten freely by slimmers. In addition, leafy vegetables provide cellulose (especially when eaten raw). So try to serve vegetables at least once a day, preferably twice, with an extra helping of raw vegetables at one meal. The vitamin C content of vegetables can be destroyed in preparation and cooking, but by eating raw vegetables you can ensure that you obtain this elusive vitamin in reasonable quantities.

Even cooked vegetables should be steamed or boiled for the shortest possible cooking time to retain their goodness and taste.

Fats All fats are high in calories, so when slimming you must be careful about the amount of fats which you eat. But don't be tempted to try and cut out fats altogether as they also provide important nutrients. About $\frac{1}{3}$ oz. of butter each day is about right, bearing in mind that protein foods supply some fat.

Cereals and starches Starches and sugars together make up carbohydrates. Such items as rice, wheat and corn are starchy. Certain vegetables belong in this group, too—peas, butter beans, potatoes and parsnips. Any food which is made from the above should also be cut down, e.g. pasta, biscuits, bread, breakfast cereals, crisps and chips.

Here again it would be pointless and monotonous to try and cut these items out of your diet altogether. Cutting down is much easier and better than cutting out. To give up all these goods entirely would make your diet monotonous, expensive and less nutritious than it needs to be.

To make sure your diet is nutritionally sound, check your intake against this list.

Protein foods—Meat, fish, eggs, cheese, poultry, lean bacon; one serving at each of three meals. Eat liver, kidney or corned beef once a week.

Vegetables—Liberal quantities of the leafy ones. One helping of raw vegetable each day as well as at least one helping of cooked vegetables.

Fruit—Two servings each day. One of these should be a citrus fruit (orange or grapefruit) but with no added sugar.

Fat—A small helping each day, but avoid too much fried food.

Starches—One or two *small* servings each day, but not between meals, i.e. no biscuits with your morning drink.

Milk—At least $\frac{1}{2}$ pint (3 decilitres, U.S. $1\frac{1}{4}$ cups) a day.

By following these simple rules you can be sure that your slimming diet provides you with sufficient of the nutrients you require to keep healthy, fit and slim.

Useful facts and figures

Oven temperature guide

	ELECTRICITY		GAS MARK
	°F	°C	
Very cool	225	110	$\frac{1}{4}$
	250	130	$\frac{1}{2}$
Cool	275	140	1
	300	150	2
Moderate	325	170	3
	350	180	4
Moderately hot	375	190	5
	400	200	6
Hot	425	220	7
	450	230	8
Very hot	475	240	9

Note: All spoon measures in this book are level.

Notes for American users

Although each recipe has an American ingredients column, the following list gives some American equivalents or substitutes for terms used in the book.

BRITISH	AMERICAN
baking tin	baking pan
base	bottom
cocktail stick	toothpick
frying pan	skillet
greaseproof paper	wax paper
grill	broil
kitchen paper	paper towels
mixer/liquidizer	mixer/blender
muslin	cheesecloth

Note: All American cup and spoon measures are level.

Average weights for men and women (in indoor clothing)
MEN

Height (in shoes) ft. in.	Small Frame st. lb.	st. lb.	(lb.)	Medium Frame st. lb.	st. lb.	(lb.)	Large Frame st. lb.	st. lb.	(lb.)
5 2	8 0	8 8	(112–120)	8 6	9 3	(118–129)	9 0	10 1	(126–141)
5 3	8 3	8 11	(115–123)	8 9	9 7	(121–133)	9 3	10 4	(129–144)
5 4	8 6	9 0	(118–126)	8 12	9 10	(124–136)	9 6	10 8	(132–148)
5 5	8 9	9 3	(121–129)	9 1	9 13	(127–139)	9 9	10 12	(135–152)
5 6	8 12	9 7	(124–133)	9 4	10 3	(130–143)	9 12	11 2	(138–156)
5 7	9 2	9 11	(128–137)	9 8	10 7	(134–147)	10 2	11 7	(142–161)
5 8	9 6	10 1	(132–141)	9 12	10 12	(138–152)	10 7	11 12	(147–166)
5 9	9 10	10 5	(136–145)	10 2	11 2	(142–156)	10 11	12 2	(151–170)
5 10	10 0	10 10	(140–150)	10 6	11 6	(146–160)	11 1	12 6	(155–174)
5 11	10 4	11 0	(144–154)	10 10	11 11	(150–165)	11 5	12 11	(159–179)
6 0	10 8	11 4	(148–158)	11 0	12 2	(154–170)	11 10	13 2	(164–184)
6 1	10 12	11 8	(152–162)	11 4	12 7	(158–175)	12 0	13 7	(168–189)
6 2	11 2	11 13	(156–167)	11 8	12 12	(162–180)	12 5	13 12	(173–194)
6 3	11 6	12 3	(160–171)	11 13	13 3	(167–185)	12 10	14 3	(178–199)
6 4	11 10	12 7	(164–175)	12 4	13 8	(172–190)	13 0	14 8	(182–204)

WOMEN

Height (in shoes) ft. in.	Small Frame st. lb.	st. lb.	(lb.)	Medium Frame st. lb.	st. lb.	(lb.)	Large Frame st. lb.	st. lb.	(lb.)
4 10	6 8	7 0	(92– 98)	6 12	7 9	(96–107)	7 6	8 7	(104–119)
4 11	6 10	7 3	(94–101)	7 0	7 12	(98–110)	7 8	8 10	(106–122)
5 0	6 12	7 6	(96–104)	7 3	8 1	(101–113)	7 11	8 13	(109–125)
5 1	7 1	7 9	(99–107)	7 6	8 4	(104–116)	8 0	9 2	(112–128)
5 2	7 4	7 12	(102–110)	7 9	8 7	(107–119)	8 3	9 5	(115–131)
5 3	7 7	8 1	(105–113)	7 12	8 10	(110–122)	8 6	9 8	(118–134)
5 4	7 10	8 4	(108–116)	8 1	9 0	(113–126)	8 9	9 12	(121–138)
5 5	7 13	8 7	(111–119)	8 4	9 4	(116–130)	8 13	10 2	(125–142)
5 6	8 2	8 11	(114–123)	8 8	9 9	(120–135)	9 3	10 6	(129–146)
5 7	8 6	9 1	(118–127)	8 12	9 13	(124–139)	9 7	10 10	(133–150)
5 8	8 10	9 5	(122–131)	9 2	10 3	(128–143)	9 11	11 0	(137–154)
5 9	9 0	9 9	(126–135)	9 6	10 7	(132–147)	10 1	11 4	(141–158)
5 10	9 4	10 0	(130–140)	9 10	10 11	(136–151)	10 5	11 9	(145–163)
5 11	9 8	10 4	(134–144)	10 0	11 1	(140–155)	10 9	12 0	(149–168)
6 0	9 12	10 8	(138–148)	10 4	11 5	(144–159)	10 13	12 5	(153–173)

(Metropolitan Life Insurance Company Statistical Bulletin)

Body-weight conversion tables

lb.	kg.	stones (lb.)	kg.
1	0.454	1 (14)	6.350
2	0.907	2 (28)	12.701
3	1.361	3 (42)	19.051
4	1.814	4 (56)	25.402
5	2.268	5 (70)	31.752
6	2.723	6 (84)	38.102
7	3.175	7 (98)	44.453
8	3.629	8 (112)	50.803
9	4.082	9 (126)	57.154
10	4.536	10 (140)	63.504
11	4.990	11 (154)	69.854
12	5.442	12 (168)	76.205
13	5.897	13 (182)	82.555
14	6.350	14 (196)	88.906
		15 (210)	95.256
		16 (224)	101.606
		17 (238)	107.957
		18 (252)	114.307
		19 (266)	120.658
		20 (280)	127.008

(Servier Laboratories Limited)

A doctor's view on why we over-eat

Doctors are unanimous in their opinion that overweight can cause ill health. Bad eating habits, often formed during childhood, are frequently responsible for obesity in later years. It is estimated that approximately 40 per cent of the adult population are overweight today, a cause for some concern.

Knowledge of food values has become much more widespread because of the interest generated by magazines and newspapers. Doctors consulted about weight problems are ready to help as much as possible by recommending diets low in calories. They are conscious of the fact that obesity is a contributing factor in causing many diseases, the most common being high blood pressure, heart disease and chronic bronchitis

There are few drugs which can be prescribed for reducing weight. There are drugs which dull the appetite, but these can only be used for a limited period as their effectiveness soon wears off.

Most important is an alteration in the whole eating pattern of the patient. A regular controlled diet is better than a crash diet if a continual loss of weight is to be achieved.

Basically a high protein diet is considered most beneficial as the nutritional value obtained from foods like meat, fish, butter, cheese, eggs and milk contain all that the body requires to remain healthy. Salads are also good and a large salad with mayonnaise used sparingly is satisfying without containing too many calories. A very limited amount of bread, preferably wholemeal, is considered good also, as this helps to give energy and provides roughage.

Many children are overweight and school doctors are concerned with this problem. School meals are considered more carefully nowadays and an effort is made to ensure that children are given a nourishing and filling lunch without too large a carbohydrate content. Dental decay, often caused by eating too many sweets, puddings and ice creams, is common among school children; another reason why sweet foods should be avoided.

Social functions are often the cause of increased weight. Businessmen, who have to do a great deal of entertaining, find it difficult to control their calorie intake. Alcohol is a great cause of trouble and men at the height of their career, around the age of say forty-five to fifty, are particularly vulnerable to heart attacks, thus suggesting that weight is definitely a contributing factor in this disease. This particular group of people probably suffer from lack of exercise, although it is not necessarily people in sedentary occupations who are obese. Manual workers can be too fat as exercise can stimulate the appetite, and again if the wrong food is eaten to satisfy this a similar result will be achieved. However, it is generally agreed that manual workers should be allowed a greater calorie intake to compensate for the energy used.

Some special foods are produced to provide meals which are filling and also low in calories. Biscuits, soups and drinks which constitute a whole meal are mass produced, and are approved by doctors providing they are taken in accordance with the instructions on the container. However they are generally rather expensive.

It cannot be stressed clearly enough that over-eating is bad and that a good eating pattern is necessary for really good health and vitality.

Starters

Whether for entertaining or for family meals, the first course can often be a problem. You are probably limiting yourself to around 1000 calories a day and so often starters are rich enough to use up a fair proportion of these calories. In fact, most people find it easier to give up the first course rather than the dessert, but I know there are times when a first course is essential.

I have chosen the recipes in this chapter with two thoughts in mind. I have made them low in calories and many can make good lunch-time snacks on their own. Much more interesting than a crispbread and a chunk of cheese!

If you are making soup, some grated cheese sprinkled over your portion turns it into a complete lunch. Your family can have their soup as a starter in the evening.

Of course, if someone special or the boss is coming to dinner, then a starter is essential, but bear in mind my advice about balancing the meal out properly. A rich starter always means a low-calorie sweet.

Yogurt prawn cocktail

Serves 2
115 calories per serving

Imperial	Metric	American
¼ pint tomato juice	1½ decilitres tomato juice	⅔ cup tomato juice
2 tablespoons lemon juice	2 tablespoons lemon juice	3 tablespoons lemon juice
salt and pepper	salt and pepper	salt and pepper
dash Worcestershire sauce	dash Worcestershire sauce	dash Worcestershire sauce
1 (5 oz.) carton natural yogurt	1 (150 g.) carton natural yogurt	1 (5 oz.) carton natural yogurt
4 oz. prawns	100 g. prawns	⅔ cup prawns or shrimp
chopped lettuce	chopped lettuce	chopped lettuce
lemon wedges	lemon wedges	lemon wedges

Mix all the ingredients together except the prawns and lettuce. Arrange a layer of lettuce in the bottom of two serving dishes, then a layer of prawns and another layer of lettuce. Top with the dressing and serve well chilled with wedges of lemon.

Crunchy baked grapefruit

Serves 2
135 calories per serving

Imperial	Metric	American
1 medium grapefruit	1 medium grapefruit	1 medium grapefruit
½ oz. butter	15 g. butter	1 tablespoon butter
½ oz. soft brown sugar	15 g. soft brown sugar	1 tablespoon soft brown sugar
½ oz. high protein breakfast cereal	15 g. high protein breakfast cereal	½ cup high protein breakfast cereal

Cut the grapefruit in half. With a sharp knife, cut round each segment to loosen it. Place the halves, cut-side up, in a shallow baking tin. Put the butter and sugar in a small pan and heat gently until melted. Remove from the heat and stir in the cereal. Mix lightly together. Sprinkle a tablespoon of the mixture over each grapefruit half.

Bake in a moderately hot oven (400°F., 200°C., Gas Mark 6) for 7–10 minutes. Serve hot.

Avocado hors d'oeuvre with yogurt dressing

Illustrated in colour on page 19
Serves 2
150 calories per serving

Imperial	Metric	American
1 avocado pear	1 avocado pear	1 avocado
juice ½ lemon	juice ½ lemon	juice ½ lemon
1 grapefruit	1 grapefruit	1 grapefruit
2 medium tomatoes	2 medium tomatoes	2 medium tomatoes
for the yogurt dressing:	**for the yogurt dressing:**	**for the yogurt dressing:**
1 (5 oz.) carton natural yogurt	1 (150 g.) carton natural yogurt	1 (5 oz.) carton natural yogurt
2 teaspoons tomato purée	2 teaspoons tomato purée	2 teaspoons tomato paste
seasoning	seasoning	seasoning

Peel, halve and slice the avocado pear and dip the slices in lemon juice. Peel the grapefruit and cut into segments. Remove the skins from the tomatoes, deseed and slice them. Divide the ingredients between two glass dishes. Serve with yogurt dressing which is made by mixing together the yogurt, tomato purée and seasoning.

Down Under savoury pears

Serves 2
89 calories per serving

Imperial	Metric	American
¾ oz. sultanas	20 g. sultanas	2 tablespoons seedless white raisins
½ small green pepper	½ small green pepper	½ small green sweet pepper
½ teaspoon grated onion	½ teaspoon grated onion	½ teaspoon grated onion
2 oz. cottage cheese	50 g. cottage cheese	¼ cup cottage cheese
salt and pepper	salt and pepper	salt and pepper
1 ripe pear	1 ripe pear	1 ripe pear
little lemon juice	little lemon juice	little lemon juice
paprika pepper	paprika pepper	paprika pepper
to garnish:	**to garnish:**	**to garnish:**
watercress	watercress	watercress

Chop the sultanas and put in a bowl. Remove the seeds and pith from the green pepper. Finely chop the flesh and add to the sultanas. Mix in the onion, cottage cheese, salt and pepper thoroughly. Cut the pear in half lengthwise and remove the core with a teaspoon. Carefully, using the teaspoon, remove the flesh of the pear to within ¼ inch (½ cm.) of the skin. Brush the edge with lemon juice.

Chop the flesh and add to the cheese mixture. Pile into the pear halves. Sprinkle with a little paprika pepper and garnish with watercress.

Grapefruit salad mould

Serves 2
122 calories per serving

Imperial	Metric	American
1 (8 oz.) can grapefruit segments	1 (225 g.) can grapefruit segments	1 (8 oz.) can grapefruit segments
½ oz. gelatine, dissolved in 2 tablespoons water	15 g. gelatine, dissolved in 2 tablespoons water	2 envelopes gelatin, dissolved in 3 tablespoons water
½ red-skinned apple, cored and chopped	½ red-skinned apple, cored and chopped	½ red-skinned apple, cored and chopped
½ teaspoon lemon juice	½ teaspoon lemon juice	½ teaspoon lemon juice
1 stick celery, chopped	1 stick celery, chopped	1 stalk celery, chopped

Drain the grapefruit and make the juice up to a scant ½ pint (¼ litre, U.S. 1 cup) with water. Add the dissolved gelatine. When nearly at setting point, add the remaining ingredients. Turn into individual moulds and allow to set.

This is also delicious served with cold chicken as a main course.

Melon and cucumber in buttermilk dressing

Serves 2
106 calories per serving

Imperial	Metric	American
1 very small ripe melon (not honeydew)	1 very small ripe melon (not honeydew)	1 very small ripe melon (not honeydew)
¼ cucumber	¼ cucumber	¼ cucumber
4 fl. oz. buttermilk	125 millilitres buttermilk	½ cup buttermilk
½ teaspoon powdered ginger	½ teaspoon powdered ginger	½ teaspoon powdered ginger

Cut the melon in half. Remove the seeds, then scoop out the flesh. Reserve the shells. Cut the flesh into cubes. Dice the cucumber and add to the melon in a mixing bowl.

Stir the buttermilk and ginger together. Pour over the fruit and leave to marinate in the refrigerator. Spoon into the melon shells when ready to serve.

Mushroom hors d'oeuvre

Serves 2
42 calories per serving

Imperial	Metric	American
4 oz. button mushrooms	100 g. button mushrooms	1 cup button mushrooms
1 (5 oz.) carton natural yogurt	1 (150 g.) carton natural yogurt	1 (5 oz.) carton natural yogurt
½ tablespoon lemon juice	½ tablespoon lemon juice	½ tablespoon lemon juice
¼ clove garlic, crushed finely	¼ clove garlic, crushed finely	¼ clove garlic, crushed finely
1 tablespoon chopped parsley	1 tablespoon chopped parsley	1 tablespoon chopped parsley
½ tablespoon chopped chives	½ tablespoon chopped chives	½ tablespoon chopped chives
salt and pepper	salt and pepper	salt and pepper

Combine all the ingredients. Leave the washed mushrooms to marinate for at least 4 hours before serving.

Tomato appetizer

Serves 2
65 calories per serving

Imperial	Metric	American
1 (8 oz.) can natural tomato juice	1 (225 g.) can natural tomato juice	1 (8 oz.) can natural tomato juice
1 (5 oz.) carton natural yogurt	1 (150 g.) carton natural yogurt	1 (5 oz.) carton natural yogurt
2–3 drops Worcestershire sauce	2–3 drops Worcestershire sauce	2–3 drops Worcestershire sauce

Mix together all the ingredients in a cocktail shaker or screw-topped jar. Shake well. Chill. Serve in glasses with ice cubes.

Slimmers' egg mayonnaise

Serves 2
110 calories per serving

Imperial	Metric	American
2 hard-boiled eggs	2 hard-boiled eggs	2 hard-cooked eggs
$\frac{1}{2}$ (5 oz.) carton natural yogurt	$\frac{1}{2}$ (150 g.) carton natural yogurt	$\frac{1}{2}$ (5 oz.) carton natural yogurt
1 gherkin, chopped	1 gherkin, chopped	1 sweet dill pickle, chopped
$1\frac{1}{2}$ tablespoons chopped chives	$1\frac{1}{2}$ tablespoons chopped chives	2 tablespoons chopped chives
1 tablespoon chopped watercress	1 tablespoon chopped watercress	1 tablespoon chopped watercress
salt and pepper	salt and pepper	salt and pepper

Cut the eggs into half lengthwise. Place in a dish. Combine the remaining ingredients, season to taste and pour over the eggs just before serving.

Jellied tomato consommé

Serves 2
45 calories per serving

Imperial	Metric	American
2 teaspoons gelatine	2 teaspoons gelatine	2 teaspoons gelatin
$2\frac{1}{2}$ tablespoons boiling water	$2\frac{1}{2}$ tablespoons boiling water	3 tablespoons boiling water
$\frac{1}{2}$ pint tomato juice	3 decilitres tomato juice	$1\frac{1}{4}$ cups tomato juice
1 small onion	1 small onion	1 small onion
strip lemon peel	strip lemon peel	strip lemon peel
2 tablespoons lemon juice	2 tablespoons lemon juice	3 tablespoons lemon juice
1 teaspoon Worcestershire sauce	1 teaspoon Worcestershire sauce	1 teaspoon Worcestershire sauce
to garnish:	**to garnish:**	**to garnish:**
chopped parsley	chopped parsley	chopped parsley

Sprinkle the gelatine into the boiling water and stir until dissolved. Pour the tomato juice into a saucepan, then add the finely chopped onion and lemon peel. Allow to come just to the boil. Strain. Add the dissolved gelatine, lemon juice and Worcestershire sauce. Leave to cool and then chill until set. Spoon into small bowls, sprinkle with parsley and serve.

Bortsch

Serves 2
91 calories per serving

Imperial	Metric	American
1 medium onion	1 medium onion	1 medium onion
1 teaspoon oil	1 teaspoon oil	1 teaspoon oil
2 (5 oz.) beetroots	2 (150 g.) beetroots	2 (5 oz.) beets
3 oz. cabbage	75 g. cabbage	3 oz. cabbage
$\frac{1}{2}$ beef stock cube, dissolved in $\frac{3}{4}$ pint water	$\frac{1}{2}$ beef stock cube, dissolved in scant $\frac{1}{2}$ litre water	$\frac{1}{2}$ beef bouillon cube, dissolved in 2 cups water
1 tablespoon vinegar	1 tablespoon vinegar	1 tablespoon vinegar
large pinch salt	large pinch salt	large dash salt
pepper	pepper	pepper
natural yogurt	natural yogurt	natural yogurt

Chop the onion finely and cook gently in the oil in a large saucepan until soft. This should take about 7 minutes. Remove the outside skin from the beetroot, chop roughly and add to the onion. Shred the cabbage finely and add to the onion and beetroot. Add the stock, vinegar, salt and pepper. Bring to the boil and simmer for about $\frac{3}{4}$ hour with the lid on the pan. Rub through a sieve, then return to the pan and reheat.

If the soup is too thick, add water to give a pouring consistency. Place a spoonful of yogurt in the centre of each helping just before serving.

Chilled green pepper soup

Serves 2
39 calories per serving

Imperial	Metric	American
1 green pepper	1 green pepper	1 green sweet pepper
$\frac{1}{2}$ chicken stock cube, dissolved in $\frac{3}{4}$ pint water	$\frac{1}{2}$ chicken stock cube, dissolved in scant $\frac{1}{2}$ litre water	$\frac{1}{2}$ chicken bouillon cube, dissolved in 2 cups water
$\frac{1}{2}$ teaspoon chopped chervil	$\frac{1}{2}$ teaspoon chopped chervil	$\frac{1}{2}$ teaspoon chopped chervil
$\frac{1}{4}$ teaspoon freshly chopped tarragon	$\frac{1}{4}$ teaspoon freshly chopped tarragon	$\frac{1}{4}$ teaspoon freshly chopped tarragon
$\frac{1}{2}$ (5 oz.) carton natural yogurt	$\frac{1}{2}$ (150 g.) carton natural yogurt	$\frac{1}{2}$ (5 oz.) carton natural yogurt

Wash the green pepper, remove the seeds and chop the flesh finely. Place in a large saucepan with the stock and herbs. Bring to the boil and simmer gently for 1 hour.

At the end of the cooking time, cool slightly and whisk in the yogurt. Liquidize to a purée or sieve several times. Place in the refrigerator to chill and serve cold.

Darwin chilled carrot and apple soup

Serves 2
25 calories per serving

Imperial	Metric	American
2 oz. new carrots, sliced	50 g. new carrots, sliced	2 small new carrots, sliced
$\frac{1}{2}$ (8 oz.) can tomatoes	$\frac{1}{2}$ (225 g.) can tomatoes	$\frac{1}{2}$ (8 oz.) can tomatoes
1 oz. apple, sliced	25 g. apple, sliced	$\frac{1}{2}$ medium apple, sliced
$\frac{1}{4}$ pint liquid, strained from tomatoes and water	$1\frac{1}{2}$ decilitres liquid, strained from tomatoes and water	$\frac{2}{3}$ cup liquid, strained from tomatoes and water
salt and pepper	salt and pepper	salt and pepper
artificial sweetener to taste	artificial sweetener to taste	artificial sweetener to taste
to garnish:	**to garnish:**	**to garnish:**
chives	chives	chives

Mix all the ingredients together and put into an electric blender. Switch to medium speed and run for 2½–3 minutes.

Adjust the seasoning and serve very cold, garnished with chopped chives.

Egg and lemon soup

Serves 4
96 calories per serving

Imperial	Metric	American
2 pints chicken stock	generous 1 litre chicken stock	5 cups chicken stock
2 oz. Patna rice	50 g. Patna rice	generous ⅓ cup Patna rice
3 eggs	3 eggs	3 eggs
juice 1 lemon	juice 1 lemon	juice 1 lemon
1 tablespoon cold water	1 tablespoon cold water	1 tablespoon cold water

Put the stock and rice into a pan, bring to the boil and allow to simmer for about 10 minutes. Beat together in a basin the eggs, lemon juice and water. Whisk in one ladleful of hot stock. Gradually add two more then pour all back into the pan. Stir well and reheat, but do not allow to boil.

Lebanese soup

Serves 2
132 calories per serving

Imperial	Metric	American
½ cucumber	½ cucumber	½ cucumber
salt	salt	salt
1 (5 oz.) carton natural yogurt	1 (150 g.) carton natural yogurt	1 (5 oz.) carton natural yogurt
2 oz. shrimps	50 g. shrimps	⅓ cup shrimp or prawns
1 teaspoon chopped chives	1 teaspoon chopped chives	1 teaspoon chopped chives
1 teaspoon chopped parsley	1 teaspoon chopped parsley	1 teaspoon chopped parsley
freshly ground pepper	freshly ground pepper	freshly ground pepper
3 tablespoons single cream	3 tablespoons single cream	scant ¼ cup coffee cream

Grate the peeled cucumber into a bowl, add the salt and leave for 5 minutes. Mix in the yogurt, shrimps, chives, parsley and pepper. Add the cream and chill. Serve with slices of cucumber.

Main dishes

Everyone needs protein. The harder you work the more protein you need. Most of our protein is eaten in the form of meat and fish—in fact the main meal provides most of our daily protein. Unfortunately meat tends to be high in calories, so the secret is to provide meat and fish dishes with lots of flavour and not too many sauces.

Cheaper cuts of meat and fish are just as nutritious as the more expensive cuts. Admittedly they need more care in preparing and cooking, but the finished result usually has plenty of flavour and will not need thickeners or flavourings added—again helping to keep down the calorie count. Try adding something different to your favourite casserole recipe, a tablespoon of pearl barley, for instance, gives a nutty flavour and also helps to thicken the gravy, without additional flour.

For a more special flavour, a little red wine or cider, added just before the end of the cooking time, makes a world of difference—remember to allow for the additional calories though.

Offal, such as liver and tripe, can be made into tasty meals for the family and are rich in vitamins and minerals. Most dietitians recommend that for children, liver should be served at least once a week.

With a little ingenuity, even today's 'convenience' foods can be dressed up to provide a main meal which will keep your family adequately nourished and slim.

Savoury fish casserole

Serves 2
279 calories per serving

Imperial	Metric	American
12 oz. filleted haddock or cod	350 g. filleted haddock or cod	¾ lb. filleted haddock or cod
1 oz. butter	25 g. butter	2 tablespoons butter
juice 1 small lemon	juice 1 small lemon	juice 1 small lemon
pepper	pepper	pepper
½ green pepper	½ green pepper	½ green sweet pepper
2 oz. mushrooms	50 g. mushrooms	½ cup mushrooms
1 small onion	1 small onion	1 small onion
1 small can tomatoes	1 small can tomatoes	1 small can tomatoes

Remove the skin from the fish and cut the fish into two portions. Brown quickly in the butter in a frying pan and then transfer to a small ovenproof dish. Sprinkle with the lemon juice and pepper. Cover the fish with the chopped pepper and chopped mushrooms, mixed together with the chopped onion. Cover the casserole well with a lid or foil and bake in a moderately hot oven (375°F., 190°C., Gas Mark 5) for 30 minutes.

Remove from the oven and add the canned tomatoes, then return to the oven for a few minutes.

Oven fried fish

Serves 2
166 calories per serving

Imperial	Metric	American
4 tablespoons low fat milk	4 tablespoons low fat milk	⅓ cup low fat milk
salt and pepper	salt and pepper	salt and pepper
dash Worcestershire sauce	dash Worcestershire sauce	dash Worcestershire sauce
½ oz. dry breadcrumbs	15 g. dry breadcrumbs	2–3 tablespoons dry bread crumbs
pinch dry mustard	pinch dry mustard	dash dry mustard
pinch cayenne pepper	pinch cayenne pepper	dash cayenne pepper
2 (4 oz.) cod steaks	2 (100 g.) cod steaks	2 (4 oz.) cod steaks
½ oz. butter, melted	15 g. butter, melted	1 tablespoon melted butter

Mix the milk with salt, pepper and Worcestershire sauce. On a separate plate, mix the breadcrumbs, dry mustard and cayenne pepper. Dip the fish first into the milk mixture and then into the crumbs.

Grease a shallow baking dish with a very little of the butter. Arrange the fish in this. Pour the remainder of the butter over the fish and bake in a moderately hot oven (400°F., 200°C., Gas Mark 6) for 30 minutes.

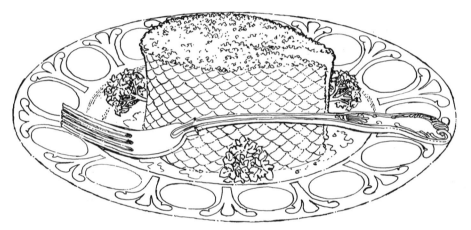

Apple fish bake

Serves 2
150 calories per serving

Imperial	Metric	American
1 small onion	1 small onion	1 small onion
1 stick celery	1 stick celery	1 stalk celery
½ small green pepper	½ small green pepper	½ small green sweet pepper
¼ oz. butter	½ tablespoon butter	½ tablespoon butter
¼ (8 oz.) can tomatoes	¼ (225 g.) can tomatoes	¼ (8 oz.) can tomatoes
little stock (made from a stock cube)	little stock (made from a stock cube)	little stock (made from a bouillon cube)
½ dessert apple	½ dessert apple	½ eating apple
2 (4 oz.) fresh or frozen cod steaks	2 (100 g.) fresh or frozen cod steaks	2 (4 oz.) fresh or frozen cod steaks
salt and pepper	salt and pepper	salt and pepper

Chop the onion, celery and green pepper. Cook gently in a non-stick pan with the butter for 5 minutes. Add the drained tomatoes and stock and cook for 10 minutes. Transfer to an ovenproof dish. Core and dice the apple and add to the dish.

Place the cod steaks on top, season well and spoon some of the mixture over the fish. Bake in a moderate oven (350°F., 180°C., Gas Mark 4) for 30 minutes.

Stuffed mackerel

Serves 2
358 calories per serving

Imperial	Metric	American
2 (6 oz.) mackerel	2 (175 g.) mackerel	2 (6 oz.) mackerel
salt and pepper	salt and pepper	salt and pepper
½ tablespoon melted butter	½ tablespoon melted butter	½ tablespoon melted butter
for the stuffing:	**for the stuffing:**	**for the stuffing:**
3 oz. fresh breadcrumbs	75 g. fresh breadcrumbs	1½ cups soft bread crumbs
½ teaspoon finely grated lemon rind	½ teaspoon finely grated lemon rind	½ teaspoon finely grated lemon rind
1 teaspoon chopped parsley	1 teaspoon chopped parsley	1 teaspoon chopped parsley
pinch mixed herbs	pinch mixed herbs	dash mixed herbs
1 egg, beaten	1 egg, beaten	1 egg, beaten
to garnish:	**to garnish:**	**to garnish:**
lemon butterflies	lemon butterflies	lemon butterflies

Wash the cleaned mackerel and sprinkle the insides with salt and pepper. Brush the outsides with melted butter.

For the stuffing, mix together the crumbs, lemon rind, parsley, herbs and egg; add sufficient water to bind. Fill the mackerel with the stuffing and grill for 5 minutes on each side. Garnish the fish with lemon butterflies and serve with mustard.

Stuffed baked salmon

Serves 2
380 calories per serving

Imperial	Metric	American
2 (4 oz.) salmon steaks, ½ inch thick	2 (100 g.) salmon steaks, 1 cm. thick	2 (4 oz.) salmon steaks, ½ inch thick
1 (2½ oz.) packet frozen prawns (reserve 4)	1 (65 g.) packet frozen prawns (reserve 4)	1 (2½ oz.) package frozen prawns (reserve 4)
½ teaspoon finely chopped parsley	½ teaspoon finely chopped parsley	½ teaspoon finely chopped parsley
1 oz. breadcrumbs	25 g. breadcrumbs	½ cup fresh bread crumbs
salt, pepper, nutmeg and mace	salt, pepper, nutmeg and mace	salt, pepper, nutmeg and mace
½ egg, beaten	½ egg, beaten	½ egg, beaten
1 oz. butter	25 g. butter	2 tablespoons butter
to garnish:	**to garnish:**	**to garnish:**
4 slices cucumber, ½ inch thick	4 slices cucumber, 1 cm. thick	4 slices cucumber, ½ inch thick
reserved prawns	reserved prawns	reserved prawns

Remove the bones from the centre of the salmon steaks. Mix the finely chopped prawns, parsley, breadcrumbs and seasoning together and bind with the beaten egg. Fill the centre of the salmon steaks with the stuffing. Butter a sheet of aluminium foil and wrap around the fish. Remove the centre from the cucumber slices with a small cutter. Place the cucumber in the foil and bake with the fish in a moderate oven (350°F., 180°C., Gas Mark 4) for 20 minutes.

Remove the fish and cucumber from the foil. Place a prawn in the centre of each cucumber slice. Serve with green salad.

Avocado hors d'oeuvre with yogurt dressing (page 11)

Fish rolls with grapes

Serves 2
186 calories per serving

Imperial	Metric	American
4 fillets plaice (3 oz. each)	4 fillets plaice (75 g. each)	4 fillets sole (3 oz. each)
seasoning	seasoning	seasoning
juice ½ lemon	juice ½ lemon	juice ½ lemon
1 golden stock cube	1 golden stock cube	1 chicken bouillon cube
¼ pint hot water	1½ decilitres hot water	⅔ cup hot water
2 tablespoons dry white wine	2 tablespoons dry white wine	3 tablespoons dry white wine
4 oz. grapes	100 g. grapes	¼ lb. grapes
to garnish:	**to garnish:**	**to garnish:**
lemon twists	lemon twists	lemon twists

Skin the fillets and roll up from the tail end. Place the rolls on their sides in a greased ovenproof dish. Season and add the lemon juice and stock, made by dissolving the cube in the hot water and dry white wine. Cover with buttered paper and place in the centre of a moderate oven (350°F., 180°C., Gas Mark 4) for 20 to 30 minutes.

When cooked, remove and strain the fish liquid into a saucepan. Boil fairly rapidly until reduced by half. This can be thickened with a little flour and butter, or left as it is. Add the grapes, pips removed, and pour the sauce over the fish. Garnish.

Boeuf stroganoff

Serves 2
248 calories per serving

Imperial	Metric	American
1 oz. margarine	25 g. margarine	2 tablespoons margarine
1 medium onion	1 medium onion	1 medium onion
2 oz. mushrooms	50 g. mushrooms	½ cup mushrooms
1 (4 oz.) grilling steak, cut into 1-inch strips	1 (100 g.) grilling steak, cut into 2½-cm. strips	1 (4 oz.) broiling steak, cut into 1-inch strips
salt and pepper	salt and pepper	salt and pepper
½ (5 oz.) carton natural yogurt	½ (150 g.) carton natural yogurt	½ (5 oz.) carton natural yogurt
lemon juice	lemon juice	lemon juice

Melt the margarine in the pan and fry the chopped onion and sliced mushrooms until soft. Add the steak and sauté gently for 5 minutes. Season and add the yogurt and a squeeze of lemon juice. Simmer for 1 minute.

Serve with green salad or green vegetables.

Liver with orange slices

Serves 2
404 calories per serving

Imperial	Metric	American
8 oz. lambs' or calves' liver	225 g. lambs' or calves' liver	½ lb. lamb or calf liver
seasoned flour	seasoned flour	seasoned flour
¾ oz. butter	20 g. butter	1½ tablespoons butter
1 teaspoon oil	1 teaspoon oil	1 teaspoon oil
1 small onion	1 small onion	1 small onion
1 clove garlic	1 clove garlic	1 clove garlic
a little stock	a little stock	a little stock
1 tablespoon red wine	1 tablespoon red wine	1 tablespoon red wine
few drops Tabasco pepper sauce	few drops Tabasco pepper sauce	few drops Tabasco pepper sauce
1 orange	1 orange	1 orange
olive oil	olive oil	olive oil
brown sugar	brown sugar	brown sugar
chopped parsley	chopped parsley	chopped parsley

Trim the liver and cut into four slices. Dip the slices in flour, well seasoned with salt, pepper, cayenne pepper and a little dry mustard. Shake off any surplus. Melt half the butter with a teaspoon of oil to prevent it burning, and fry the liver for a minute or two. Turn the liver and cook the other side. Remove to a hot serving dish and keep warm. Add the rest of the butter and cook the finely chopped onion and very finely chopped garlic in this until soft. Then add the stock and wine. Simmer until reduced a little and then add the Tabasco pepper sauce. Adjust the seasoning if necessary.

Pour over the liver and serve with the orange slices. To make these, peel and slice the orange, brush with oil, sprinkle with brown sugar and quickly heat through under the grill. Sprinkle with parsley and serve.

Paprika beef

Serves 2
440 calories per serving

Imperial	Metric	American
1 tablespoon oil	1 tablespoon oil	1 tablespoon oil
1 onion	1 onion	1 onion
8 oz. chuck steak	225 g. chuck steak	½ lb. chuck steak
1 tablespoon paprika pepper	1 tablespoon paprika pepper	1 tablespoon paprika pepper
1 (8 oz.) can tomatoes	1 (225 g.) can tomatoes	1 (8 oz.) can tomatoes
1 tablespoon tomato purée	1 tablespoon tomato purée	1 tablespoon tomato paste
bay leaf	bay leaf	bay leaf
4 tablespoons red wine	4 tablespoons red wine	⅓ cup red wine
salt and pepper	salt and pepper	salt and pepper

Heat the oil in a pan and sauté the peeled and sliced onion until tender but not brown. Cut the steak into pieces and brown in the oil. Dissolve the paprika pepper in a little hot water and add to the meat. Add the canned tomatoes and tomato purée and stir well. Add the bay leaf, wine and seasoning. Place in a casserole, cover and cook for 1½–2 hours at 350°F., 180°C., Gas Mark 4, or until the meat is tender. Add a little water if necessary during cooking.

Ragoût of kidneys

Serves 2
215 calories per serving

Imperial	Metric	American
8 oz. pigs' or veal kidneys	225 g. pigs' or veal kidneys	½ lb. pork or veal kidneys
salt and pepper	salt and pepper	salt and pepper
1 beef stock cube	1 beef stock cube	1 beef bouillon cube
½ pint hot water	3 decilitres hot water	1¼ cups hot water
1 oz. mushrooms	25 g. mushrooms	¼ cup mushrooms
1 tablespoon oil	1 tablespoon oil	1 tablespoon oil
½ tablespoon chopped onion	½ tablespoon chopped onion	½ tablespoon chopped onion
½ oz. flour	15 g. flour	2 tablespoons flour

Remove the core, fat and fine skin from the kidneys. Slice the kidneys and sprinkle with salt and pepper. Crumble the beef stock cube in the hot water. Wash and slice the mushrooms.

Heat half the oil and fry the kidney slices in it for about 3 minutes. Remove from the pan. Add the rest of the oil, heat and fry the onion until brown and cooked. Sprinkle in the flour and mix well. Cook for a minute and then add the stock. Stir until it boils. Add the mushrooms and the kidneys and simmer until the mushrooms are cooked.

Tripe provençale

Serves 2
105 calories per serving

Imperial	Metric	American
½ tablespoon oil	½ tablespoon oil	½ tablespoon oil
½ medium onion	½ medium onion	½ medium onion
1 stick celery	1 stick celery	1 stalk celery
½ green pepper	½ green pepper	½ green sweet pepper
¼ (8 oz.) can tomatoes	¼ (225 g.) can tomatoes	¼ (8 oz.) can tomatoes
4 oz. prepared tripe	100 g. prepared tripe	¼ lb. fresh prepared tripe
¼ pint stock (using a chicken stock cube)	1½ decilitres stock (using a chicken stock cube)	⅔ cup stock (using a chicken bouillon cube)
pinch marjoram	pinch marjoram	dash marjoram
salt and pepper	salt and pepper	salt and pepper
½ tablespoon cornflour	½ tablespoon cornflour	½ tablespoon cornstarch
1 tablespoon cold water	1 tablespoon cold water	1 tablespoon cold water
¼ pint low fat milk	1½ decilitres low fat milk	⅔ cup low fat milk

Heat the oil in a non-stick saucepan. Add the chopped onion, chopped celery and chopped green pepper and cook gently until soft. Add the drained tomatoes, tripe—cut into small pieces, stock, herbs and seasoning. Cover and cook for about 1 hour over a gentle heat.

Mix the cornflour with the water, blend in the milk and pour into the stew. Bring to the boil, stirring all the time, and cook for 5 minutes until the sauce begins to thicken. Adjust seasoning and serve at once.

Chicken curry

Illustrated in colour on opposite page
Serves 2
250 calories per serving (excluding side dishes)

Imperial	Metric	American
½ (5 oz.) carton natural yogurt	½ (150 g.) carton natural yogurt	½ (5 oz.) carton natural yogurt
1 clove garlic	1 clove garlic	1 clove garlic
2 (6 oz.) chicken joints	2 (175 g.) chicken joints	2 (6 oz.) chicken joints
½ tablespoon butter	½ tablespoon butter	½ tablespoon butter
1 small onion	1 small onion	1 small onion
½ tablespoon curry powder	½ tablespoon curry powder	½ tablespoon curry powder
1 cooking apple	1 cooking apple	1 baking apple
salt and pepper	salt and pepper	salt and pepper
½ teaspoon cornflour	½ teaspoon cornflour	½ teaspoon cornstarch
scant ½ pint chicken stock	¼ litre chicken stock	1 cup chicken stock
chopped parsley	chopped parsley	chopped parsley

Mix the yogurt and crushed garlic in a soup plate and marinate the chicken in it for a few hours, turning frequently.

Heat the butter in a non-stick pan and fry the chopped onion until soft. Add the curry powder and cook for 2–3 minutes. Add the peeled and chopped apple, drained chicken pieces, salt and pepper. Mix the cornflour with the stock, add to the pan and stir. Cover and cook for about 1 hour or until the chicken is tender. Stir in the yogurt, reheat and sprinkle with chopped parsley. Serve with side dishes of sliced bananas in lemon juice, diced eating apple in lemon juice, sliced tomatoes and onion rings and mango chutney.

Remember that rice is for non-slimmers!

Liver shashlik

Serves 2
167 calories per serving

Imperial	Metric	American
8 oz. calves' liver	225 g. calves' liver	½ lb. calf liver
1 medium onion	1 medium onion	1 medium onion
4 medium tomatoes	4 medium tomatoes	4 medium tomatoes
4 oz. mushrooms	100 g. mushrooms	1 cup mushrooms
fresh bay leaves	fresh bay leaves	fresh bay leaves
1 tablespoon oil	1 tablespoon oil	1 tablespoon oil
little vinegar	little vinegar	little vinegar
salt and pepper	salt and pepper	salt and pepper
chopped parsley	chopped parsley	chopped parsley
juice ½ lemon	juice ½ lemon	juice ½ lemon

Wash the liver in warm water and remove any coarse tubes. Cut into slices 1½ inches (3½ cm.) thick. Dry on kitchen paper. Peel and slice the onion, cut the tomatoes in quarters, wash the mushrooms and cut in half if large. Wash the bay leaves. Take four long skewers and thread the ingredients in the following order—bay leaf, liver, mushroom, tomato, onion, repeating these until all the ingredients are used. Place in the bottom of a grill pan and brush with oil. Sprinkle with a little vinegar and season with salt and pepper. Leave to marinate for ½ hour.

Grill the meat skewers for 10 minutes. Remove to a hot dish. Add a little water to the grill pan to make a gravy. Transfer to a small saucepan and boil hard to reduce. Add the parsley and lemon juice and pour over the meat.

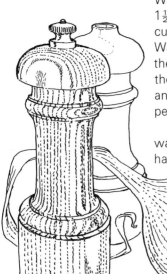
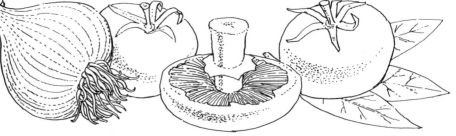

Beef olives

Serves 2
411 calories per serving

Imperial	Metric	American
8 oz. lean stewing steak	225 g. lean stewing steak	½ lb. piece lean beef stew meat
½ (4 oz.) packet savoury stuffing mix	½ (100 g.) packet savoury stuffing mix	½ (4 oz.) package savory stuffing mix
1 small onion	1 small onion	1 small onion
1 carrot	1 carrot	1 carrot
½ beef stock cube	½ beef stock cube	½ beef bouillon cube
¼ pint hot water	1½ decilitres hot water	⅔ cup hot water
½ tablespoon oil	½ tablespoon oil	½ tablespoon oil
1 bay leaf	1 bay leaf	1 bay leaf
salt and pepper	salt and pepper	salt and pepper

Ask your butcher to slice the meat into thick pieces about 4 × 3 inches (10 × 7½ cm.) or do this yourself with a very sharp knife. Place on a board and beat well to flatten. Prepare the stuffing, spread some on to each piece of meat. Roll up the slices of meat and secure with thick cotton or fine string. Peel and slice the onion and carrot. Dissolve the stock cube in the hot water. Heat the oil in a pan and cook the onion for a few minutes, add the beef olives and brown on each side. Add the carrot, bay leaf and stock. Season. Cover and simmer until tender, removing the thread or string before serving with the unthickened gravy and a green vegetable.

Farmhouse chicken

Serves 2
356 calories per serving

Imperial	Metric	American
2 chicken portions	2 chicken portions	2 chicken pieces
little seasoned flour	little seasoned flour	little seasoned flour
½ tablespoon oil	½ tablespoon oil	½ tablespoon oil
1 onion	1 onion	1 onion
2 carrots	2 carrots	2 carrots
½ green pepper	½ green pepper	½ green sweet pepper
½ stock cube	½ stock cube	½ bouillon cube
⅓ pint hot water	2–2½ decilitres hot water	generous ¾ cup hot water
seasoning	seasoning	seasoning
small pinch tarragon	small pinch tarragon	small dash tarragon
½ small carton single cream or top of the milk	½ small carton single cream or top of the milk	½ small carton coffee cream
to garnish:	**to garnish:**	**to garnish:**
green pepper	green pepper	green sweet pepper
chopped parsley	chopped parsley	chopped parsley

Coat the chicken with seasoned flour and fry quickly to seal the meat. Transfer to a casserole. Fry the chopped onion, sliced carrots and sliced green pepper in the oil and add these to the chicken. Make up the stock by adding the stock cube to the hot water. Pour this stock over the vegetables and chicken, season and add the tarragon. Cook in the oven, with the lid on the casserole, for 1½ hours at 350°F., 180°C., Gas Mark 4.

When cooked, remove the chicken joints and place on to a serving dish. Add the cream to the vegetables and stock and pour this sauce over the chicken.

Garnish with slivers of green pepper and freshly chopped parsley.

Savoury lamb hot pot

This dish couldn't be simpler to make, it owes a lot of its flavour to the clever use of herbs.
Serves 2
348 calories per serving

Imperial	Metric	American
1 medium onion	1 medium onion	1 medium onion
6 oz. lean lamb	175 g. lean lamb	⅓ lb. lean lamb
4 oz. potatoes	100 g. potatoes	¼ lb. potatoes
½ (8 oz.) can tomatoes	½ (225 g.) can tomatoes	½ (8 oz.) can tomatoes
scant ½ pint stock (using a stock cube)	¼ litre stock (using a stock cube)	1 cup stock (using a bouillon cube)
salt and pepper	salt and pepper	salt and pepper
pinch marjoram	pinch marjoram	dash marjoram
pinch basil	pinch basil	dash basil
chopped parsley	chopped parsley	chopped parsley

Peel and slice the onion and place in a casserole. Trim any fat from the lamb, cut it into bite-sized pieces and add to the casserole. Top with sliced potatoes and drained tomatoes. Add the stock, season well with salt, pepper and herbs.

Bake in a moderate oven (325°F., 170°C., Gas Mark 3) for 1¼ hours, adding a little water during cooking if there are any signs of drying out.

Salads and Vegetable dishes

Salads and raw vegetables need no introduction to the slimmer. Far from it! The slimmer is very likely to say 'Not salads again!'. But this is what this chapter is all about. Salads need not be boring and vegetables can be turned into delicious hot meals. Just try these recipes for size!

The trouble is that so often we think of a salad as being a mixture of lettuce, tomato, cucumber and a hard-boiled egg, with the odd radish added for decoration. There are, in fact, hundreds of different items which can be added to a salad to give it interest, flavour and texture.

For instance, a little cold chicken mixed with shredded lettuce or chicory and a chopped fresh peach makes a delicious and substantial salad with a difference. Cottage cheese can be given 'bite' by adding a few chopped walnuts.

Try mixing fresh fruit with vegetables and aim for different textures. I expect you add raisins to an apple pie, so why not make a salad with fresh chopped apple, cottage cheese and raisins with lemon juice or yogurt.

Presentation is important. Always make sure the vegetables are fresh and crisp and the fruit is ripe without being mushy.

Remember fruit and vegetables are not only low in calories, they are also high in vitamin and mineral content, so everyone should have at least two helpings every day. This way you not only make sure you lose weight, but you ensure that you and your family stay fit and get the extra benefits of strong nails, shiny hair and clear skin, too.

And for those of you who can't resist nibbling between meals—nibble on raw vegetables instead of biscuits. Keep a bowl of celery fingers, carrot fingers, washed radishes and cucumber cubes in the fridge. After a while you may find the family enjoying them as much as sweets or cakes.

Salads

Orange and cauliflower salad

Illustrated in colour on opposite page
Serves 4
135 calories per serving

Imperial	Metric	American
½ cauliflower	½ cauliflower	½ cauliflower
1 orange	1 orange	1 orange
2 sticks celery	2 sticks celery	2 stalks celery
½ eating apple	½ eating apple	½ eating apple
½ onion	½ onion	½ onion
lemon juice	lemon juice	lemon juice
4 oz. Edam cheese	100 g. Edam cheese	¼ lb. Edam cheese

Divide the cauliflower into florets, wash thoroughly and mix with the peeled and skinned orange segments. Add the chopped celery, grated apple and onion, cut into thin rings. Toss the salad in the lemon juice and add the cubed cheese.

Orange and cauliflower salad

Canberra coleslaw medley

Serves 2
231 calories per serving

Imperial	Metric	American
6 oz. white cabbage, shredded	175 g. white cabbage, shredded	1½–2 cups shredded white cabbage
2 tablespoons pineapple pieces	2 tablespoons pineapple pieces	3 tablespoons pineapple pieces
1 dessert apple	1 dessert apple	1 eating apple
1 stick celery	1 stick celery	1 stalk celery
1 eating pear	1 eating pear	1 eating pear
4 tablespoons mayonnaise	4 tablespoons mayonnaise	⅓ cup mayonnaise
lettuce leaves	lettuce leaves	lettuce leaves
2 black olives, stoned	2 black olives, stoned	2 ripe olives, pitted
2 green olives, stoned	2 green olives, stoned	2 green olives, pitted
2 walnuts	2 walnuts	2 walnuts
parsley	parsley	parsley
watercress	watercress	watercress

Crisp the cabbage in cold water for ½ hour. Dry. Combine the cabbage, drained pineapple pieces, cored and sliced apple, sliced celery and cored and sliced pear with the mayonnaise, making sure all the ingredients are coated. Line a salad bowl with lettuce leaves. Tip the mixture into this and garnish with olives, chopped walnuts, chopped parsley and watercress. This is delicious with cold chicken.

Devilled eggs with crispy salad

Serves 2
257 calories per serving

Imperial	Metric	American
4 eggs, hard-boiled	4 eggs, hard-boiled	4 eggs, hard-cooked
½ tablespoon mayonnaise	½ tablespoon mayonnaise	½ tablespoon mayonnaise
1 teaspoon curry powder	1 teaspoon curry powder	1 teaspoon curry powder
4 oz. cabbage	100 g. cabbage	¼ lb. cabbage
4 oz. carrots	100 g. carrots	¼ lb. carrots
½ stick celery	½ stick celery	½ stalk celery
½ green pepper	½ green pepper	½ green sweet pepper
1 red eating apple	1 red eating apple	1 red eating apple

Cut the eggs in half lengthways, remove the yolks. Sieve the yolks and mix with the mayonnaise and curry powder. Beat well and pipe back into the white halves. Slice the cabbage, grate the carrots and chop the celery. Deseed and slice the pepper and core and slice the apple. Mix all these together, pile on to a serving dish. Arrange the stuffed eggs on top.

Balkan salad

Serves 2
368 calories per serving

Imperial	Metric	American
1 packet frozen green beans	1 packet frozen green beans	1 package frozen green beans
½ small onion	½ small onion	½ small onion
½ oz. margarine	15 g. margarine	1 tablespoon margarine
1 oz. blanched almonds	25 g. blanched almonds	¼ cup blanched almonds
2 oz. raisins	50 g. raisins	⅓ cup raisins
for the dressing:	**for the dressing:**	**for the dressing:**
pinch salt and pepper	pinch salt and pepper	dash salt and pepper
pinch dry mustard	pinch dry mustard	dash dry mustard
1 tablespoon vinegar	1 tablespoon vinegar	1 tablespoon vinegar
2 tablespoons oil	2 tablespoons oil	3 tablespoons oil

Cook the green beans according to the instructions on the packet. Drain well and cut the beans in half. Fry the sliced onion in the margarine until soft. Shred the almonds and add to the onion with the raisins. Continue frying until the almonds and onion are light golden brown, then remove from the pan and allow to cool before adding the beans. Chill for ½ hour.

Make up the dressing by adding the seasonings to the vinegar and oil and shaking in a screw topped bottle. Toss the mixture in the dressing and serve.

Crudités apple salad

Serves 2
300 calories per serving

Imperial	Metric	American
½ small cauliflower	½ small cauliflower	½ small cauliflower
6 spring onions	6 spring onions	6 scallions
2 new carrots	2 new carrots	2 new carrots
1 red dessert apple	1 red dessert apple	1 red eating apple
2 tablespoons lemon juice	2 tablespoons lemon juice	3 tablespoons lemon juice
few stuffed olives	few stuffed olives	few stuffed olives
4 oz. salami, sliced	100 g. salami, sliced	¼ lb. salami, sliced
2 small tomatoes, halved	2 small tomatoes, halved	2 small tomatoes, halved

Break the cauliflower into small sprigs, cut the tops off the spring onions and soak the carrots, cut into 2-inch (5-cm.) sticks, in ice cold water for 30 minutes to crisp. Core and thinly slice the apple and toss the slices in the lemon juice to prevent discolouration. Attractively arrange all the ingredients on two plates. Sprinkle French dressing over, if liked, before serving.

Pacific pear and salmon salad

Serves 2
270 calories per serving

Imperial	Metric	American
pinch salt, pepper, dry mustard and sugar	pinch salt, pepper, dry mustard and sugar	dash salt, pepper, dry mustard and sugar
2 tablespoons corn oil	2 tablespoons corn oil	3 tablespoons corn oil
1 tablespoon white wine	1 tablespoon white wine	1 tablespoon white wine
1 (7 oz.) can red salmon	1 (200 g.) can red salmon	1 (7 oz.) can red salmon
1 ripe pear	1 ripe pear	1 ripe pear
2 tablespoons capers	2 tablespoons capers	3 tablespoons capers
few lettuce leaves	few lettuce leaves	few lettuce leaves
chopped chives	chopped chives	chopped chives

Blend the seasonings with the oil in a medium-sized bowl. Add the wine gradually, beating well with a fork. Add the drained salmon. Mix the peeled, cored and diced pear with the capers and add to the salmon, mixing well. Arrange lettuce leaves on two plates. Place half the salad on each plate and sprinkle with chives. Chill a little before serving.

Rollmop Waldorf salad

Serves 2
282 calories per serving

Imperial	Metric	American
1 apple	1 apple	1 apple
1 stick celery	1 stick celery	1 stalk celery
½ oz. walnuts, chopped	15 g. walnuts, chopped	2 tablespoons chopped walnuts
1 teaspoon chopped chervil, parsley or basil	1 teaspoon chopped chervil, parsley or basil	1 teaspoon chopped chervil, parsley or basil
½ (5 oz.) carton natural yogurt	½ (150 g.) carton natural yogurt	½ (5 oz.) carton natural yogurt
2 (3 oz.) herring rollmops	2 (75 g.) herring rollmops	2 (3 oz.) herring rollmops

Mix the cored and chopped apple, chopped celery, walnuts and herbs with the yogurt. Unroll the rollmops. Spread each with the mixture and then re-roll. Chill well. Serve with any salad vegetables.

Tuna summer salad

Serves 2
285 calories per serving

Imperial	Metric	American
1 tablespoon chopped gherkins	1 tablespoon chopped gherkins	1 tablespoon chopped sweet dill pickles
1 tablespoon grated radish	1 tablespoon grated radish	1 tablespoon grated radish
1 tablespoon chopped spring onion	1 tablespoon chopped spring onion	1 tablespoon chopped scallion
1 tablespoon lemon juice	1 tablespoon lemon juice	1 tablespoon lemon juice
½ teaspoon Worcestershire sauce	½ teaspoon Worcestershire sauce	½ teaspoon Worcestershire sauce
1 (7 oz.) can tuna fish	1 (200 g.) can tuna fish	1 (7 oz.) can tuna fish
1 (8 oz.) carton cottage cheese	1 (225 g.) carton cottage cheese	1 (8 oz.) carton cottage cheese
salt and pepper	salt and pepper	salt and pepper

Mix the gherkins, radish, spring onion, lemon juice and Worcestershire sauce together. Flake the tuna fish with a fork and mix with the cottage cheese. Blend the two mixtures together well and season.
    Serve with blanched, sliced green pepper.

Fruity ham salad

Serves 2
137 calories per serving

Imperial	Metric	American
3 oz. piece lean ham	75 g. piece lean ham	3 oz. piece lean cooked ham
1 dessert apple	1 dessert apple	1 eating apple
juice ½ lemon	juice ½ lemon	juice ½ lemon
½ tablespoon mayonnaise	½ tablespoon mayonnaise	½ tablespoon mayonnaise
½ tablespoon Piccalilli	½ tablespoon Piccalilli	½ tablespoon Piccalilli relish
salt and pepper	salt and pepper	salt and pepper

Cut the ham into cubes. Wash and core the apple, cut into dice and sprinkle with lemon juice. Mix the mayonnaise and Piccalilli with the seasoning and toss with the apple and ham. Chill and serve.

Pineapple ice cream and Crêpes aux pêches (pages 35 and 67)

Salad dressings

Watercress dressing

This dressing is best made at least ½ hour before serving.
83 calories for this dressing

Imperial	Metric	American
½ bunch watercress	½ bunch watercress	½ bunch watercress
1 (5 oz.) carton natural yogurt	1 (150 g.) carton natural yogurt	1 (5 oz.) carton natural yogurt
½ teaspoon lemon juice	½ teaspoon lemon juice	½ teaspoon lemon juice
salt and pepper	salt and pepper	salt and pepper

Remove any coarse stalks from the watercress, chop the rest very finely. Mix with the yogurt and lemon juice. Season to taste.

Mint dressing

75 calories for this dressing

Imperial	Metric	American
1 (5 oz.) carton natural yogurt	1 (150 g.) carton natural yogurt	1 (5 oz.) carton natural yogurt
1 tablespoon finely chopped fresh mint	1 tablespoon finely chopped fresh mint	1 tablespoon finely chopped fresh mint
salt and pepper	salt and pepper	salt and pepper

Combine the yogurt and mint. Season to taste.

Danish blue dressing

281 calories for this dressing

Imperial	Metric	American
2 oz. Danish blue cheese	50 g. Danish blue cheese	2 oz. Danish blue cheese
1 (5 oz.) carton natural yogurt	1 (150 g.) carton natural yogurt	1 (5 oz.) carton natural yogurt

Crumble the cheese finely and stir into the yogurt.

Vegetable dishes

Italian cauliflower

Serves 4
230 calories per serving

Imperial	Metric	American
1 (1½ lb.) medium cauliflower	1 (700 g.) medium cauliflower	1 (1½ lb.) medium cauliflower
1 medium onion	1 medium onion	1 medium onion
½ clove garlic	½ clove garlic	½ clove garlic
½ oz. butter	15 g. butter	1 tablespoon butter
1 (8 oz.) can tomatoes	1 (225 g.) can tomatoes	1 (8 oz.) can tomatoes
salt and pepper	salt and pepper	salt and pepper
½ pint white sauce	3 decilitres white sauce	1¼ cups white sauce
2 oz. Parmesan cheese, grated	50 g. Parmesan cheese, grated	½ cup grated Parmesan cheese
to garnish:	**to garnish:**	**to garnish:**
4 black olives	4 black olives	4 ripe olives

Cook the cauliflower in boiling salted water until just tender, then drain well. Chop the onion finely and cook with the crushed garlic in the melted butter until soft. Add the drained tomatoes and cook for 10 minutes.

Put the cauliflower, whole, into a baking dish and surround it with the tomato and onion mixture. Coat with the seasoned white sauce. Sprinkle Parmesan cheese over the dish and brown in a hot oven (425°F., 220°C., Gas Mark 7). Serve garnished with black olives.

Aubergine with tomatoes

Serves 2
100 calories per serving

Imperial	Metric	American
1 aubergine	1 aubergine	1 eggplant
salt	salt	salt
1 small onion	1 small onion	1 small onion
½ tablespoon olive oil	½ tablespoon olive oil	½ tablespoon olive oil
½ (8 oz.) can tomatoes	½ (225 g.) can tomatoes	½ (8 oz.) can tomatoes
pinch mixed herbs	pinch mixed herbs	dash mixed herbs
2 anchovy fillets	2 anchovy fillets	2 anchovy fillets
½ oz. Parmesan cheese, grated	15 g. Parmesan cheese, grated	2 tablespoons grated Parmesan cheese

Cut the aubergine in half lengthways. Score across with a knife. Sprinkle with salt and leave for 30 minutes. Wrap in foil and bake in a moderate oven for 45 minutes or so, until soft. Meanwhile, sauté the sliced onion in the oil, add the drained tomatoes and herbs and cook for 15 minutes. Scoop out the flesh from the aubergine, add to the pan with the tomato mixture and mix together.

Refill each aubergine half and top with an anchovy fillet. Sprinkle with Parmesan cheese and bake for a further 15 minutes.

Ratatouille

This is a delicious vegetable dish which can be served hot or cold, on its own or as an accompaniment to a main dish.
Serves 2
119 calories per serving

Imperial	Metric	American
1 aubergine	1 aubergine	1 eggplant
4 oz. courgettes	100 g. courgettes	¼ lb. small zucchini
1 tablespoon olive oil	1 tablespoon olive oil	1 tablespoon olive oil
½ green pepper	½ green pepper	½ green sweet pepper
1 small onion	1 small onion	1 small onion
½ clove garlic	½ clove garlic	½ clove garlic
½ (8 oz.) can tomatoes	½ (225 g.) can tomatoes	½ (8 oz.) can tomatoes
salt and pepper	salt and pepper	salt and pepper

Slice the aubergine and courgettes and fry lightly in oil. Add the sliced green pepper, onion, crushed garlic and drained tomatoes. Season well.
Cover and cook for about 1 hour until all the vegetables are tender.

Sweet and sour red cabbage

Serves 2
57 calories per serving

Imperial	Metric	American
12 oz. red cabbage	350 g. red cabbage	¾ lb. red cabbage
½ dessert apple	½ dessert apple	½ eating apple
½ teaspoon cornflour	½ teaspoon cornflour	½ teaspoon cornstarch
1 tablespoon cider vinegar	1 tablespoon cider vinegar	1 tablespoon cider vinegar
liquid artificial sweetener	liquid artificial sweetener	liquid artificial sweetener
salt and pepper	salt and pepper	salt and pepper

Shred the red cabbage and cook it in a little water with the chopped apple, for about 10 minutes. Mix the cornflour with the cider vinegar and artificial sweetener and stir into the cabbage and apple mixture. Bring to the boil and simmer gently for another 10–15 minutes. Taste and adjust seasoning.

Desserts

If you have a sweet tooth, probably the worst part of slimming is the feeling that you must say goodbye to desserts of any sort other than fruit or water ices. This need not necessarily be true, if you follow some of the recipes in this chapter.

Make full use of artificial sweeteners and powdered low fat milk when cooking desserts. They reduce the calorie count considerably.

It is quite possible, of course, to live and eat well and at the same time cut out desserts. We eat far more sugar in this country than in any other (excepting the U.S.A.) and a great deal of this sugar is consumed in the form of desserts.

The Continentals prefer fresh fruit to finish off a meal. I think the trick here is to present your family with a selection of fruit, nicely arranged. Just putting an apple or orange in front of them takes the glitter away, but if you arrange a peach and a few grapes on a leaf in a saucer or glass dish, it looks delicious and the family will love it.

There is no time of the year now when fresh fruit is not readily available in all parts of the country; so there is no excuse on that score for making roly-poly puddings and suchlike. I know they are delicious but they do add on inches where you can least afford to add them! Try serving fresh strawberries with lemon juice instead of sugar and cream. I assure you the combination of flavours is surprisingly good.

If you have a home freezer, then you are lucky because you can freeze soft fruits in season and make delicious desserts just when you need them. Alternatively, you can buy frozen fruit at any freezer market. Almost any fresh fruit, except bananas, will fit in well with a slimming diet—but I do mean fresh fruit not canned, which has a much higher calorie content!

Spiced oranges

Serves 2
50 calories per serving

Imperial	Metric	American
2 oranges	2 oranges	2 oranges
$\frac{1}{4}$ pint water	$1\frac{1}{2}$ decilitres water	$\frac{2}{3}$ cup water
pinch cinnamon	pinch cinnamon	dash cinnamon
nutmeg	nutmeg	nutmeg
liquid artificial sweetener	liquid artificial sweetener	liquid artificial sweetener

Peel the oranges and remove any pith. Cut into slices and place in a saucepan with the rest of the ingredients. Bring to the boil and simmer for 2–3 minutes. Chill before serving.

Tangy apple fluff

Serves 2
98 calories per serving

Imperial	Metric	American
2 dessert apples	2 dessert apples	2 eating apples
juice $\frac{1}{2}$ lemon	juice $\frac{1}{2}$ lemon	juice $\frac{1}{2}$ lemon
1 tablespoon redcurrant jelly	1 tablespoon redcurrant jelly	1 tablespoon red currant or similar jelly
1 egg white	1 egg white	1 egg white
little ground cinnamon	little ground cinnamon	little ground cinnamon

Peel and core the apples, chop roughly and cook in a little water until mushy. Sieve and add the lemon juice and redcurrant jelly. Cool and fold in the stiffly beaten egg white. Sprinkle with a little ground cinnamon and chill well before serving.

Rhubarb jelly

Serves 2
16 calories per serving

Imperial	Metric	American
8 oz. rhubarb (cut into 1-inch pieces)	225 g. rhubarb (cut into $2\frac{1}{2}$-cm. pieces)	$\frac{1}{2}$ lb. rhubarb (cut into 1-inch pieces)
$\frac{1}{8}$ pint low-calorie undiluted lemon squash	4 tablespoons low-calorie undiluted lemon squash	$\frac{1}{3}$ cup low-calorie undiluted lemon drink
curl lemon rind	curl lemon rind	curl lemon rind
3 artificial sweetener tablets	3 artificial sweetener tablets	3 artificial sweetener tablets
$\frac{1}{4}$ oz. powdered gelatine	1 tablespoon powdered gelatine	1 envelope powdered gelatin

Stew the rhubarb in the lemon squash, with the curl of lemon rind. Sweeten to taste. Allow to cool slightly. Dissolve the gelatine with 2 tablespoons water or according to packet instructions and stir into the mixture. Pour into a mould and allow to set. Serve with fresh fruit or cream.

Pineapple ice cream

Illustrated in colour on page 31
Serves 4
97 calories per serving

Imperial	Metric	American
1 large pineapple (about $1\frac{1}{2}$ lb.)	1 large pineapple (about 700 g.)	1 large pineapple (about $1\frac{1}{2}$ lb.)
5 drops liquid artificial sweetener	5 drops liquid artificial sweetener	5 drops liquid artificial sweetener
$\frac{1}{4}$ pint natural yogurt	$1\frac{1}{2}$ decilitres natural yogurt	$\frac{2}{3}$ cup natural yogurt

Cut the top off the pineapple, leaving about 1 inch ($2\frac{1}{2}$ cm.) of the fruit attached to the leaves to form a lid. Scrape out the pulp from the body of the pineapple without damaging the case. Remove any core. Purée this pulp and mix it with the artificial sweetener and yogurt.

Pour into a freezing tray and put into the ice box of a refrigerator turned to the coldest setting. When the mixture is slushy, mash or whisk it to break down the large crystals. Return to the icebox until it is frozen. When ready to serve, quickly spoon it into the pineapple case.

Oeufs à la neige

Serves 2
171 calories per serving

Imperial	Metric	American
½ pint low fat milk	3 decilitres low fat milk	1¼ cups low fat milk
liquid artificial sweetener	liquid artificial sweetener	liquid artificial sweetener
few drops vanilla essence	few drops vanilla essence	few drops vanilla extract
2 egg whites	2 egg whites	2 egg whites
pinch salt	pinch salt	dash salt
1 tablespoon castor sugar	1 tablespoon castor sugar	1 tablespoon sugar
2 egg yolks	2 egg yolks	2 egg yolks

Bring the milk to the boil and stir in the sweetener and vanilla essence. Beat the egg whites and salt until very stiff and fold in the castor sugar. Divide the meringue mixture into four and drop each portion into the boiling milk and cook for 2–3 minutes. Turn the 'meringues' over and cook for another few minutes. Remove with a strainer and put on one side.

Beat the egg yolks, add a drop of sweetener and gradually add the hot milk, stirring all the time to prevent curdling. Cook over a very gentle heat, stirring until the mixture thickens. Chill. Divide into two dishes and serve with the meringues.

Yogurt parfait

Serves 2
120 calories per serving

Imperial	Metric	American
artificial sweetener to taste	artificial sweetener to taste	artificial sweetener to taste
1 (5 oz.) carton natural yogurt	1 (150 g.) carton natural yogurt	1 (5 oz.) carton natural yogurt
1 ripe pear	1 ripe pear	1 ripe pear
1 orange	1 orange	1 orange
½ small melon	½ small melon	½ small melon

Sweeten the yogurt if liked and place a little in the base of two sundae glasses. Peel, core and chop the pear, peel and chop the orange. Remove the seeds from the melon and spoon out the flesh or use a melon baller. Arrange a few pieces of fruit on top of the yogurt and then add more yogurt. Continue in layers until the glasses are full.

Decorate with strawberry halves if in season or a piece of the orange and serve chilled.

Pear, grape and strawberry cups

Serves 2
69 calories per serving

Imperial	Metric	American
¼ pint strong low-calorie lemon squash	1½ decilitres strong low-calorie lemon squash	⅔ cup strong low-calorie lemon drink
rind ½ lemon	rind ½ lemon	rind ½ lemon
little yellow food colouring	little yellow food colouring	little yellow food coloring
1 pear	1 pear	1 pear
3 oz. black grapes	75 g. black grapes	3 oz. purple grapes
4 oz. strawberries	100 g. strawberries	¼ lb. strawberries

Make up the lemon squash, add the lemon rind and a little yellow colouring. Peel, core and slice the pear and remove the grape pips. Place all the fruits in a bowl. Pour the juice over the fruit. Chill thoroughly and serve piled into sundae glasses.

Orange fruit baskets

Serves 2
80 calories per serving
(without sugar)

Imperial	Metric	American
2 large oranges	2 large oranges	2 large oranges
2 oz. strawberries	50 g. strawberries	scant ½ cup strawberries
2 oz. dark red cherries	50 g. dark red cherries	scant ½ cup Bing cherries
little castor sugar, if liked	little castor sugar, if liked	little sugar, if liked
few drops maraschino	few drops maraschino	few drops maraschino
1 (5–6-inch) piece angelica	1 (13–15-cm.) piece angelica	1 (5–6-inch) piece candied angelica

Cut across the oranges about a third of the way down from the top, in a zig-zag fashion. Remove the flesh, leaving a firm cup of orange skin. Remove the pips and pith from the flesh and chop the flesh. Mix the halved strawberries, halved and stoned cherries, sugar, if used, and the maraschino with any juice from the orange and refill the orange cups.

Soak the angelica in boiling water to remove any excess sugar and to soften. Cut into thin strips and curl round a rolling pin to form a handle. Secure by wrapping in aluminium foil, allow to cool and become firm. Place an angelica handle on each basket, putting the ends of the angelica well inside the orange cups.

Pineapple cheese dessert

Serves 2
124 calories per serving

Imperial	Metric	American
4 oz. canned pineapple pieces	100 g. canned pineapple pieces	1 cup canned pineapple pieces
4 oz. cottage cheese	100 g. cottage cheese	½ cup cottage cheese
2 tablespoons conc. orange juice	2 tablespoons conc. orange juice	3 tablespoons conc. orange juice

Strain the pineapple well so that no juice is left. Stir the pineapple into the cottage cheese and blend well. Add the orange juice. Mix well together and place in individual dishes. Chill before serving.

Coffee mould

Serves 2
127 calories per serving

Imperial	Metric	American
¼ pint black coffee	1½ decilitres black coffee	⅔ cup black coffee
½ oz. gelatine	15 g. gelatine	2 envelopes gelatin
½ pint milk	3 decilitres milk	1¼ cups milk
½ teaspoon vanilla essence	½ teaspoon vanilla essence	½ teaspoon vanilla extract
1–2 drops artificial sweetener	1–2 drops artificial sweetener	1–2 drops artificial sweetener
2 large egg whites	2 large egg whites	2 large egg whites

Place the black coffee and the gelatine in a small pan. Heat gently until the gelatine has dissolved. Remove from the heat and add the milk, vanilla essence and sweetener. Mix together and pour the mixture into a bowl. Allow to stand until almost set. Whisk the egg whites stiffly and fold into the mixture. Pour into a bowl or mould and chill.

Blackcurrant yogurt sorbet

Serves 2
70 calories per serving

Imperial	Metric	American
4 oz. blackcurrants	100 g. blackcurrants	1 cup blackcurrants or blueberries
1 (5 oz.) carton natural yogurt	1 (150 g.) carton natural yogurt	1 (5 oz.) carton natural yogurt
little lemon juice	little lemon juice	little lemon juice
liquid artificial sweetener, if liked	liquid artificial sweetener, if liked	liquid artificial sweetener, if liked
½ tablespoon gelatine	½ tablespoon gelatine	½ tablespoon gelatin
2 tablespoons water	2 tablespoons water	3 tablespoons water
1 egg white	1 egg white	1 egg white

Adjust your refrigerator to the lowest setting. Combine the cooked and puréed blackcurrants, yogurt and lemon juice in a bowl. Sweeten to taste. Dissolve the gelatine in water in a basin over hot water, then stir this into the purée mixture. When the mixture begins to set, fold in the stiffly beaten egg white. Pour into a shallow container and freeze.

Fruit cocktail

Serves 2
104 calories per serving

Imperial	Metric	American
1 small cooking apple	1 small cooking apple	1 small baking apple
½ grapefruit	½ grapefruit	½ grapefruit
1 orange	1 orange	1 orange
4 oz. grapes	100 g. grapes	¼ lb. grapes
1 large or 2 small egg whites	1 large or 2 small egg whites	1 large or 2 small egg whites
artificial sweetener	artificial sweetener	artificial sweetener
to decorate:	**to decorate:**	**to decorate:**
glacé cherries	glacé cherries	candied cherries

Peel and poach the cored and sliced apple in a little water until soft, then sieve well to a purée. Beat with a wooden spoon. Peel the grapefruit and cut into small pieces. Peel the orange and cut into segments. Wash the grapes and remove the skin and pips. Mix all the fruit together and place in two individual dishes.

Whisk the egg white until very stiff, fold in the apple purée gently (artificially sweeten if liked). Pile on to the fruit and decorate with a glacé cherry.

Clafoutis

Serves 2
187 calories per serving

Imperial	Metric	American
1 red-skinned apple	1 red-skinned apple	1 red-skinned apple
1 tablespoon flour	1 tablespoon flour	1 tablespoon flour
artificial sweetener to taste	artificial sweetener to taste	artificial sweetener to taste
1 egg	1 egg	1 egg
scant ½ pint milk	¼ litre milk	1 cup milk

Place the cored and chopped apple in the base of a small ovenproof dish. Cream the flour, artificial sweetener and egg together until smooth. Gradually blend in the milk and pour over the apple. Bake in a moderately hot oven (400°F., 200°C., Gas Mark 6) for 35 minutes. Allow to cool slightly before serving.

Rhubarb crumble

Serves 2
71 calories per serving

Imperial	Metric	American
8 oz. rhubarb	225 g. rhubarb	$\frac{1}{2}$ lb. rhubarb
juice scant $\frac{1}{2}$ lemon	juice scant $\frac{1}{2}$ lemon	juice scant $\frac{1}{2}$ lemon
liquid artificial sweetener	liquid artificial sweetener	liquid artificial sweetener
1 oz. fresh breadcrumbs	25 g. fresh breadcrumbs	$\frac{1}{2}$ cup fresh bread crumbs
$\frac{1}{4}$ teaspoon ground ginger	$\frac{1}{4}$ teaspoon ground ginger	$\frac{1}{4}$ teaspoon ground ginger
$\frac{1}{2}$ tablespoon butter	$\frac{1}{2}$ tablespoon butter	$\frac{1}{2}$ tablespoon butter

Cut the rhubarb into pieces and place in an ovenproof dish. Sprinkle on the lemon juice mixed with 1–2 drops of liquid sweetener. Mix the breadcrumbs with the ground ginger and sprinkle on top of the fruit. Dot with butter and bake in a moderate oven (350°F., 180°C., Gas Mark 4) for 35 minutes.

Orange custard

Serves 2
160 calories per serving

Imperial	Metric	American
2 eggs	2 eggs	2 eggs
juice and rind 1 orange	juice and rind 1 orange	juice and rind 1 orange
artificial sweetener to taste	artificial sweetener to taste	artificial sweetener to taste
$\frac{1}{2}$ pint milk (made from powdered low fat milk)	3 decilitres milk (made from powdered low fat milk)	$1\frac{1}{4}$ cups milk (made from powdered low fat milk)

Beat together the eggs, orange juice and sweetener. Pour on the scalded milk, beat well and strain into a small soufflé dish or individual moulds. Stand in a tin of water and bake in a moderate oven (350°F., 180°C., Gas Mark 4) for 40–45 minutes. Remove from the oven but allow to become cold before turning out on to a serving dish. Sprinkle the top with grated orange rind before serving.

Peach delight

Serves 2
54 calories per serving

Imperial	Metric	American
2 large fresh peaches	2 large fresh peaches	2 large fresh peaches
4 tablespoons undiluted low-calorie orange squash	4 tablespoons undiluted low-calorie orange squash	$\frac{1}{3}$ cup undiluted low-calorie orange drink
large pinch powdered ginger	large pinch powdered ginger	large dash powdered ginger
1 teaspoon finely grated orange rind	1 teaspoon finely grated orange rind	1 teaspoon finely grated orange rind
artificial sweetener	artificial sweetener	artificial sweetener

Peel the peaches and cut into quarters or segments. Arrange in the bottom of a small soufflé dish. Spoon the orange squash over the peaches and then sprinkle with the ginger and orange rind. Add the sweetener, if liked.

Cover the dish with foil and bake in a moderately hot oven (400°F., 200°C., Gas Mark 6) for about 15 minutes.

High teas and Supper dishes

Not everyone has dinner in the evening. Husbands may have had a splendid 'business' lunch and the children have school lunches; so all that is required in the evening is a high tea or supper. This can be a difficult meal for a Mum who is trying to slim, especially as children have a preference for fish fingers and chips, sausages and beans and other high-calorie dishes.

However, if you are prepared to spend a little more time preparing this meal, it is possible to cook dishes which will satisfy the family and still let you lose weight.

It is no more difficult to prepare a light savoury casserole than it is to stand over the chip pan, and the resulting dish is much tastier and much lower in calories.

Another advantage is that with a hearty meat, fish or vegetable dish there is no need to provide bread and butter or cake.

Eggs and cheese are very versatile and can be made into many delicious, low-calorie dishes. Try Eggs creole or Cheesy haddock.

Baked country supper

Serves 4
276 calories per serving

Imperial	Metric	American
8 oz. leeks	225 g. leeks	$\frac{1}{2}$ lb. leeks
4 oz. tomatoes	100 g. tomatoes	$\frac{1}{4}$ lb. tomatoes
8 oz. potatoes	225 g. potatoes	$\frac{1}{2}$ lb. potatoes
$\frac{1}{2}$ teaspoon mixed herbs	$\frac{1}{2}$ teaspoon mixed herbs	$\frac{1}{2}$ teaspoon mixed herbs
1 small can condensed chicken soup	1 small can condensed chicken soup	1 small can condensed chicken soup
salt and pepper	salt and pepper	salt and pepper
4 eggs	4 eggs	4 eggs
2 oz. cheese, grated	50 g. cheese, grated	$\frac{1}{2}$ cup grated cheese

Cut the leeks into $\frac{1}{4}$-inch ($\frac{1}{2}$-cm.) slices and cook in salted water for 10–15 minutes. Drain well. Arrange the sliced tomatoes in the bottom of a greased ovenproof dish. Mix together the leeks, cooked and diced potatoes, herbs, soup and seasoning. Place on top of the tomatoes. Make four hollows and break an egg into each. Sprinkle with grated cheese.

Bake in a moderately hot oven (375°F., 190°C., Gas Mark 5) for 12–15 minutes, until the eggs are set and the mixture well heated through.

Egg and tomato slice

Serves 2
337 calories per serving

Imperial	Metric	American
2 rashers bacon	2 rashers bacon	2 bacon slices
1 small onion	1 small onion	1 small onion
1 (8 oz.) can tomatoes, liquid retained	1 (225 g.) can tomatoes, liquid retained	1 (8 oz.) can tomatoes, liquid retained
large pinch mixed herbs	large pinch mixed herbs	large dash mixed herbs
milk and tomato juice mixed to ½ pint	milk and tomato juice mixed to 3 decilitres	milk and tomato juice mixed to 1¼ cups
2 eggs	2 eggs	2 eggs
salt and pepper	salt and pepper	salt and pepper
1 oz. cheese, grated	25 g. cheese, grated	¼ cup grated cheese

Fry the chopped bacon for a few minutes, add the finely chopped onion and cook for a further 3–4 minutes. Add the drained tomatoes and herbs, then place in an ovenproof dish. Beat together the scalded milk and juice, eggs and seasoning. Strain into the dish, cover with the cheese and bake in a moderate oven (350°F., 180°C., Gas Mark 4) for 40 minutes. Serve with vegetables.

Porky meat loaf

Serves 4
250 calories per serving

Imperial	Metric	American
4 oz. pig's liver	100 g. pig's liver	¼ lb. pork liver
2 oz. lean bacon	50 g. lean bacon	2 slices Canadian bacon
4 oz. pork sausage meat	100 g. pork sausage meat	¼ lb. pork sausage meat
½ oz. white breadcrumbs	15 g. white breadcrumbs	¼ cup white bread crumbs
salt and pepper	salt and pepper	salt and pepper
2 oz. mushrooms, finely chopped	50 g. mushrooms, finely chopped	½ cup finely chopped mushrooms
¼ teaspoon sage	¼ teaspoon sage	¼ teaspoon sage
2 teaspoons tomato chutney	2 teaspoons tomato chutney	2 teaspoons tomato chutney or relish

Trim the liver and cut the rind from the bacon, if necessary. Mince the liver and bacon and then mix them together, stirring in all the other ingredients. Mix thoroughly. Press into a basin, cover closely with foil and bake in a moderate oven (325°F., 170°C., Gas Mark 3) for 1½ hours. Leave the loaf in the basin until cold. Serve sliced with salad.

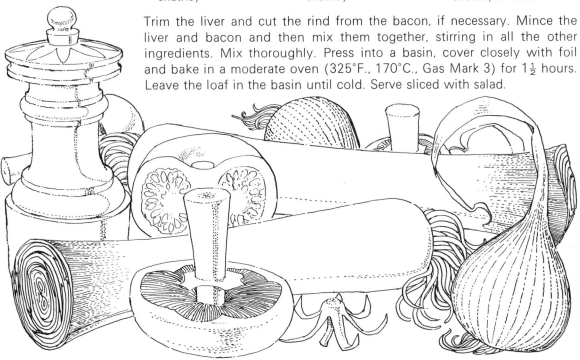

Cheese omelette

Illustrated in colour on page 51
Serves 2
280 calories per serving
(excluding salad)

Imperial	Metric	American
3 eggs	3 eggs	3 eggs
1 tablespoon water	1 tablespoon water	1 tablespoon water
$\frac{1}{2}$ teaspoon salt	$\frac{1}{2}$ teaspoon salt	$\frac{1}{2}$ teaspoon salt
$\frac{1}{2}$ oz. butter	15 g. butter	1 tablespoon butter
2 oz. Edam cheese, grated	50 g. Edam cheese, grated	$\frac{1}{2}$ cup grated Edam cheese

Beat the eggs and water until blended and add the salt. Heat the butter in a non-stick or omelette pan until it sizzles. Pour in the egg mixture and tilt the pan so that it will coat the bottom evenly. As the egg begins to set, push it towards the centre to allow the uncooked part to run underneath.

When almost cooked, sprinkle with the grated cheese. Fold the omelette over and roll on to a heated plate. Divide the omelette and serve with sliced tomatoes and a green salad.

Normandy herring fillets

Serves 2
388 calories per serving

Imperial	Metric	American
2 medium herrings	2 medium herrings	2 medium herring
seasoned flour	seasoned flour	seasoned flour
2 tablespoons melted margarine	2 tablespoons melted margarine	3 tablespoons melted margarine
1 eating apple	1 eating apple	1 eating apple
little lemon juice	little lemon juice	little lemon juice
salt and pepper	salt and pepper	salt and pepper
to garnish:	**to garnish:**	**to garnish:**
chopped parsley	chopped parsley	chopped parsley

Bone the herrings and flatten them out. Dust them well with seasoned flour and brush with the melted margarine. Grill on both sides, turning once, until tender; brushing frequently with the juices.

Peel, core and slice the apple. Poach in a little water until tender but not broken. Add the lemon juice and seasoning. Arrange the herrings on a serving dish and spoon the apple over. Garnish with chopped parsley.

Sesame fish rolls

Serves 2
261 calories per serving
without sesame seeds
178 calories per 1 oz.
(25 g.) sesame seeds

Imperial	Metric	American
2 fillets haddock	2 fillets haddock	2 fillets haddock
$\frac{1}{2}$ oz. butter	15 g. butter	1 tablespoon butter
$\frac{1}{2}$ oz. flour	15 g. flour	2 tablespoons flour
$\frac{1}{4}$ pint milk	$1\frac{1}{2}$ decilitres milk	$\frac{2}{3}$ cup milk
1 oz. Cheddar cheese, grated	25 g. Cheddar cheese, grated	$\frac{1}{4}$ cup grated Cheddar cheese
$\frac{1}{2}$ tablespoon lemon juice	$\frac{1}{2}$ tablespoon lemon juice	$\frac{1}{2}$ tablespoon lemon juice
salt and pepper	salt and pepper	salt and pepper
little mustard powder	little mustard powder	little mustard powder
1 oz. sesame seeds, toasted	25 g. sesame seeds, toasted	3 tablespoons sesame seeds, toasted

Trim the fillets and roll up. Secure with cocktail sticks. Arrange in a fireproof dish, season and add a little fish stock. Cover and bake in a moderate oven (350°F., 180°C., Gas Mark 4) for 15 minutes. Melt the butter, add the flour and gradually stir in the milk. Bring to the boil, stirring all the time. Stir in cheese, juice, seasoning and mustard.

Drain the fish and arrange in a dish. Coat with the sauce. Grill for a few minutes until the top is brown. Sprinkle with toasted sesame seeds.

Peppered eggs

Serves 2
230 calories per serving

Imperial	Metric	American
1 green pepper	1 green pepper	1 green sweet pepper
½ oz. butter	15 g. butter	1 tablespoon butter
4 oz. mushrooms, sliced	100 g. mushrooms, sliced	1 cup sliced mushrooms
2 eggs	2 eggs	2 eggs
salt and pepper	salt and pepper	salt and pepper
1 oz. cheese, grated	25 g. cheese, grated	¼ cup grated cheese

Cut the pepper in half lengthways, remove the seeds and core. Cook in boiling water for 5–6 minutes. Drain and place in an ovenproof dish. Melt the butter in a pan, add the mushrooms and cook for a few minutes until soft.

Arrange the mushrooms in the pepper cases and break an egg into each. Sprinkle with the seasoning and cheese. Bake in a moderately hot oven (375°F., 190°C., Gas Mark 5) for 15–20 minutes.

Devilled burgers

Serves 2
157 calories per serving

Imperial	Metric	American
6 oz. lean stewing steak	175 g. lean stewing steak	about ⅓ lb. lean beef stewmeat
1 small onion	1 small onion	1 small onion
½ teaspoon mustard	½ teaspoon mustard	½ teaspoon mustard
2 teaspoons Worcestershire sauce	2 teaspoons Worcestershire sauce	2 teaspoons Worcestershire sauce
1 teaspoon meat extract	1 teaspoon meat extract	1 teaspoon gravy mix powder
salt	salt	salt

Finely mince the steak and the onion. Add the mustard, Worcestershire sauce and meat extract or gravy mix powder dissolved in 3 teaspoons hot water. Season to taste with salt and mix well. Shape into 4 thin cakes. Stand them under a pre-heated grill. Grill for about 3 minutes per side. Serve with a green vegetable.

Cheesy haddock

Serves 2
215 calories per serving

Imperial	Metric	American
2 oz. Cheddar cheese, grated	50 g. Cheddar cheese, grated	½ cup grated Cheddar cheese
1 teaspoon Marmite	1 teaspoon Marmite	1 teaspoon yeast extract
pinch mixed herbs	pinch mixed herbs	dash mixed herbs
½ teaspoon Worcestershire sauce	½ teaspoon Worcestershire sauce	½ teaspoon Worcestershire sauce
½ teaspoon dry mustard	½ teaspoon dry mustard	½ teaspoon dry mustard
2 tablespoons milk	2 tablespoons milk	3 tablespoons milk
seasoning	seasoning	seasoning
2 (4 oz.) portions cod fillet	2 (100 g.) portions cod fillet	2 (4 oz.) portions cod fillet

Mix the cheese with the Marmite, herbs, Worcestershire sauce, mustard and milk. Season to taste with salt and pepper. Stand the fish in a foil-lined grill pan and grill for about 7 minutes. Turn the fish over and spread with the cheese mixture. Grill for a further 3–4 minutes, or until the cheese mixture is golden and bubbly. Serve immediately.

Cottage cheese baked potatoes

For those occasions when you just can't resist a potato — this recipe turns a potato into a nourishing and filling meal.
Serves 2
227 calories per serving

Imperial	Metric	American
2 large potatoes	2 large potatoes	2 large potatoes
salt and pepper	salt and pepper	salt and pepper
2 oz. cooked lean ham, chopped	50 g. cooked lean ham, chopped	¼ cup chopped cooked lean ham
4 oz. cottage cheese	100 g. cottage cheese	½ cup cottage cheese
1 teaspoon made mustard	1 teaspoon made mustard	1 teaspoon prepared mustard
to garnish:	**to garnish:**	**to garnish:**
watercress or sliced tomato	watercress or sliced tomato	watercress or sliced tomato

Place the potatoes in a moderately hot oven (400°F., 200°C., Gas Mark 6) and bake for about 50 minutes until cooked. Cut in half, scoop out the centre and mix with the remaining ingredients. Pile back into the potato shells and reheat for 5 minutes. Serve garnished with watercress or tomato slices.

Eggs creole

Serves 2
178 calories per serving

Imperial	Metric	American
½ tablespoon margarine	½ tablespoon margarine	½ tablespoon margarine
½ small onion	½ small onion	½ small onion
½ green pepper	½ green pepper	½ green sweet pepper
1 oz. mushrooms	25 g. mushrooms	¼ cup mushrooms
2 tomatoes	2 tomatoes	2 tomatoes
little chicken stock	little chicken stock	little chicken stock
salt and pepper	salt and pepper	salt and pepper
pinch marjoram	pinch marjoram	dash marjoram
2 eggs	2 eggs	2 eggs

Melt the margarine in a pan. Add the chopped onion and diced green pepper and gently fry till soft. Add the mushrooms, sliced, and cook for another few minutes. Mix in the skinned and chopped tomatoes and stock. Season to taste and cover. Cook gently for 15 minutes.

Break the eggs into the pan one at a time and cook over a low heat until the whites are set.

Smoked fish and cottage cheese cocottes

Serves 2
174 calories per serving

Imperial	Metric	American
4 oz. smoked haddock	100 g. smoked haddock	¼ lb. smoked haddock
4 oz. cottage cheese	100 g. cottage cheese	½ cup cottage cheese
1 small onion	1 small onion	1 small onion
2 oz. mushrooms	50 g. mushrooms	½ cup mushrooms
1 egg	1 egg	1 egg
juice ½ lemon	juice ½ lemon	juice ½ lemon
salt and pepper	salt and pepper	salt and pepper
to garnish:	**to garnish:**	**to garnish:**
lemon twists	lemon twists	lemon twists

Cook the fish in a little water for about 7 minutes until tender. Flake the fish and mix with the cottage cheese, chopped onion and chopped mushrooms. Beat the egg and add to the mixture. Add the lemon juice and season to taste. Grease two ramekin dishes or a small ovenproof dish and place the mixture in this. Stand the dish or dishes in a baking tin of warm water and cook in a moderate oven (350°F., 180°C., Gas Mark 4) for about 30 minutes or until set. Garnish with lemon twists and serve.

Welsh tomatoes

Serves 2
177 calories per serving

Imperial	Metric	American
8 oz. leeks	225 g. leeks	½ lb. leeks
½ oz. butter	15 g. butter	1 tablespoon butter
1 large tomato	1 large tomato	1 large tomato
salt and pepper	salt and pepper	salt and pepper
1 oz. Parmesan cheese	25 g. Parmesan cheese	1 oz. Parmesan cheese
1 small slice starch-reduced bread	1 small slice starch-reduced bread	1 small slice starch-reduced bread

Wash the leeks and cut off the roots and most of the green. Cut the remainder into slices and fry in the butter until soft. Add the sliced tomato and seasoning and cook for a further 5 minutes.

Turn into a fireproof dish, sprinkle on the grated Parmesan cheese and crumbled bread. Place under a hot grill until golden brown.

Cauliflower champignon

Serves 2
183 calories per serving

Imperial	Metric	American
1 (1 lb.) small cauliflower	1 (450 g.) small cauliflower	1 (1 lb.) small cauliflower
½ small can condensed cream of mushroom soup	½ small can condensed cream of mushroom soup	½ small can condensed cream of mushroom soup
1 oz. sharp Cheddar cheese	25 g. sharp Cheddar cheese	¼ cup grated sharp Cheddar cheese
salt and pepper	salt and pepper	salt and pepper
1 tablespoon starch-reduced breadcrumbs	1 tablespoon starch-reduced breadcrumbs	1 tablespoon starch-reduced bread crumbs
to garnish:	**to garnish:**	**to garnish:**
parsley or tomato slices	parsley or tomato slices	parsley or tomato slices

Cook the cauliflower in boiling, salted water, then break into good-sized flowerets and put in a shallow ovenproof dish.

While the cauliflower is cooking, combine the soup and grated cheese in a pan and heat well. Season to taste.

Pour the cheese and mushroom mixture over the cooked cauliflower. Sprinkle with breadcrumbs and brown under a hot grill. Garnish.

Kipper and mushroom en papillote

Serves 2
194 calories per serving

Imperial	Metric	American
2 kippers	2 kippers	2 kippers
2 teaspoons lemon juice	2 teaspoons lemon juice	2 teaspoons lemon juice
salt and pepper	salt and pepper	salt and pepper
4 oz. button mushrooms	100 g. button mushrooms	1 cup button mushrooms
to garnish:	**to garnish:**	**to garnish:**
lemon slices	lemon slices	lemon slices
parsley	parsley	parsley

Sprinkle the kippers, head removed, with lemon juice and season with salt and pepper. Arrange the sliced mushrooms down the centre of the kippers and enclose each kipper loosely in a piece of aluminium foil. Bake in a moderately hot oven (400°F., 200°C., Gas Mark 6) for 15 minutes.

Remove from the foil and serve garnished with lemon slices and parsley.

If you serve with 1 thin slice of Hovis or brown bread with a scraping of butter, and follow with 4 oz. (100 g.) fresh pineapple, the total calorie count for each person is 354.

Austrian stuffed cabbage

Serves 2
255 calories per serving

Imperial	Metric	American
8 oz. green cabbage	225 g. green cabbage	½ lb. green head cabbage
1 apple	1 apple	1 apple
2 oz. Cheddar cheese, grated	50 g. Cheddar cheese, grated	½ cup grated Cheddar cheese
1 oz. fresh, starch-reduced breadcrumbs	25 g. fresh, starch-reduced breadcrumbs	½ cup fresh, starch-reduced bread crumbs
salt and pepper	salt and pepper	salt and pepper
1 small egg	1 small egg	1 small egg
½ (8 oz.) can tomatoes	½ (225 g.) can tomatoes	½ (8 oz.) can tomatoes

Select two good large leaves from the cabbage or four good smaller leaves. Cut away the firm stalk and blanch the leaves in boiling water.

Mix the chopped apple, grated cheese, breadcrumbs and seasoning and bind with the beaten egg. Shape into two or four even-sized balls. Completely envelop each in cabbage leaves. Place in an ovenproof dish, pour the tomatoes on top and bake in a moderate oven (350°F., 180°C., Gas Mark 4) for 40—45 minutes.

Turkey and ham stuffed apples

Still some cold turkey left over, the family will love these for a change!
Serves 2
272 calories per serving

Imperial	Metric	American
4 oz. cooked turkey, chopped	100 g. cooked turkey, chopped	½ cup chopped cooked turkey
1 oz. lean ham, chopped	25 g. lean ham, chopped	2 tablespoons chopped cooked, lean ham
2 oz. pineapple chunks	50 g. pineapple chunks	⅓ cup pineapple chunks
3 oz. green grapes	75 g. green grapes	⅔ cup white grapes
1 stick celery	1 stick celery	1 stalk celery
2 tablespoons low-calorie mayonnaise	2 tablespoons low-calorie mayonnaise	3 tablespoons low-calorie mayonnaise
2 large apples	2 large apples	2 large apples
to decorate:	**to decorate:**	**to decorate:**
little grated lemon rind	little grated lemon rind	little grated lemon rind

Toss the turkey and ham together with the drained pineapple, seeded grapes, chopped celery and mayonnaise.

Cut the tops off the apples. Core and hollow out the flesh. Cut the flesh into small dice and add to the turkey mixture. Spoon the mixture into the apple cavities and decorate the top of each with a little grated lemon rind.

Salad meat balls

Serves 2
396 calories per serving

Imperial	Metric	American
6 oz. corned beef	175 g. corned beef	scant ⅓ lb. corned beef
2 hard-boiled eggs	2 hard-boiled eggs	2 hard-cooked eggs
2 tablespoons mayonnaise	2 tablespoons mayonnaise	3 tablespoons mayonnaise
1 teaspoon made mustard	1 teaspoon made mustard	1 teaspoon prepared mustard
salt and pepper	salt and pepper	salt and pepper
½ small packet potato crisps	½ small packet potato crisps	½ small package potato chips

Mash the corned beef well with a fork. Chop the eggs and add the corned beef, together with the mayonnaise, mustard and seasoning. Mix thoroughly and make into 6 'golf ball' shapes. Toss in the crushed potato crisps and arrange in a dish with lettuce and mustard and cress.

Recipes for the overweight male

Overweight men can be problematical, as they are not usually so figure conscious. They tend to scoff at the idea of dieting—usually referring to diets as 'living off lettuce like a rabbit'.

The fact remains, however, that many men are overweight, so the woman has the responsibility of cutting down on his calories without making it look too obvious!

Whether the man in your life's problem is caused by hearty business lunches or whether he just has a sandwich and a beer at lunch-time (too high in both calories and carbohydrates), you will have the job of providing him with at least one of his main meals. You should aim for a meal which is high in protein and low in calories and carbohydrates.

The easiest and most obvious way is to serve meat and vegetables (no potatoes) and a side salad. For instance, a grilled steak will only take about 10 minutes to prepare. If this is served with a tomato or green salad on the side, it will keep your overweight male healthy and happy and also help him slim.

Recipes in this chapter are given for all three courses; this allows you to vary the menus. Serve a starter and main dish one day and a main dish and dessert another. The more variety the better, so long as you make sure you do not let him exceed his calorie allowance for the day.

Starters

Curried pear appetizer

Serves 2
95 calories per serving

Imperial	Metric	American
2 ripe pears	2 ripe pears	2 ripe pears
1 tablespoon lemon juice	1 tablespoon lemon juice	1 tablespoon lemon juice
$\frac{1}{2}$ (5 oz.) carton natural yogurt	$\frac{1}{2}$ (150 g.) carton natural yogurt	$\frac{1}{2}$ (5 oz.) carton natural yogurt
$\frac{1}{2}$ small onion	$\frac{1}{2}$ small onion	$\frac{1}{2}$ small onion
salt and pepper	salt and pepper	salt and pepper
$\frac{1}{2}$ tablespoon curry powder	$\frac{1}{2}$ tablespoon curry powder	$\frac{1}{2}$ tablespoon curry powder
$\frac{1}{2}$ teaspoon lemon juice	$\frac{1}{2}$ teaspoon lemon juice	$\frac{1}{2}$ teaspoon lemon juice
$\frac{1}{2}$ pimento, cut in strips	$\frac{1}{2}$ pimento, cut in strips	$\frac{1}{2}$ pimiento, cut in strips
$\frac{1}{2}$ tablespoon chopped parsley	$\frac{1}{2}$ tablespoon chopped parsley	$\frac{1}{2}$ tablespoon chopped parsley

Peel and halve the pears. Remove the cores with a teaspoon and re-assemble to form whole pears. Toss in lemon juice to prevent discoloration. Mix the yogurt, grated onion, seasoning, curry powder and lemon juice. Spoon this mixture over the pears so they are completely coated.

Decorate the top of each with a cross of pimento and sprinkle parsley down the centre. Arrange on a flat dish and serve.

Liver soup

Serves 2
125 calories per serving

Imperial	Metric	American
4 oz. liver	100 g. liver	¼ lb. liver
1 pint stock, made from a stock cube	generous ½ litre stock, made from a stock cube	2½ cups stock, made from a bouillon cube
2 onions	2 onions	2 onions
4 oz. carrots	100 g. carrots	¼ lb. carrots
1 bay leaf	1 bay leaf	1 bay leaf
pinch thyme	pinch thyme	dash thyme
salt and pepper	salt and pepper	salt and pepper
gravy browning	gravy browning	gravy coloring

Cut the liver into smallish pieces. Put the liver, stock, finely chopped vegetables and herbs into a pan and bring to the boil. When the vegetables are tender, remove the bay leaf and pass the soup through a sieve or blender. Reheat and season to taste. Colour with a little gravy browning and serve sprinkled with parsley.

Pear hors d'oeuvre

Serves 2
170 calories per serving

Imperial	Metric	American
1 small lemon	1 small lemon	1 small lemon
2 fresh pears	2 fresh pears	2 fresh pears
chopped parsley	chopped parsley	chopped parsley
1 small can crab meat	1 small can crab meat	1 small can crab meat
2 tablespoons mayonnaise	2 tablespoons mayonnaise	3 tablespoons mayonnaise
seasoning	seasoning	seasoning

Cut the lemon flesh into cubes and reserve a few cubes for garnish. Halve and core the pears and sprinkle the halves with juice from the remaining lemon cubes. Cover the cut sides with chopped parsley. Mix together the crab meat and mayonnaise and season to taste. Pile on to the pear halves. Garnish with lemon cubes.

Main dishes

Fillet of sole with mushroom sauce

Serves 2
200 calories per serving

Imperial	Metric	American
2 (4 oz.) sole fillets	2 (100 g.) sole fillets	2 (4 oz.) sole fillets
½ teaspoon salt	½ teaspoon salt	½ teaspoon salt
little pepper	little pepper	little pepper
½ tablespoon margarine	½ tablespoon margarine	½ tablespoon margarine
4 oz. mushrooms	100 g. mushrooms	1 cup mushrooms
½ onion	½ onion	½ onion
3–4 tablespoons dry white wine	3–4 tablespoons dry white wine	4–5 tablespoons dry white wine
1 teaspoon flour	1 teaspoon flour	1 teaspoon flour
4 teaspoons single cream	4 teaspoons single cream	4 teaspoons coffee cream
1 tablespoon chopped parsley or few grapes	1 tablespoon chopped parsley or few grapes	1 tablespoon chopped parsley or few grapes

Sprinkle the fillets with salt and pepper. Melt the margarine and sauté half the sliced mushrooms and chopped onion for 3 minutes. Lay the seasoned fillets on top of this mixture and cover with remaining sliced mushrooms. Pour the wine over, cover and simmer very gently for 15 minutes or until the fish is white and flaky.

Mix the flour into the cream until smooth and add to the fish, stirring until thickened. Cook for 2–3 minutes. Serve with halved grapes or a sprinkling of chopped parsley.

Poached salmon with savoury sauce

Serves 2
256 calories per serving

Imperial	Metric	American
2 salmon steaks (about 4 oz. each)	2 salmon steaks (about 100 g. each)	2 salmon steaks (about ¼ lb. each)
salt and pepper	salt and pepper	salt and pepper
1 onion	1 onion	1 onion
1 stick celery	1 stick celery	1 stalk celery
scant ½ pint water	¼ litre water	1 cup water
2 egg yolks	2 egg yolks	2 egg yolks
to garnish:	**to garnish:**	**to garnish:**
thinly sliced cucumber	thinly sliced cucumber	thinly sliced cucumber
parsley	parsley	parsley

Sprinkle the salmon with salt and pepper. Put the sliced vegetables into a small saucepan with the fish on top, and add the water. Bring to the boil, cover and cook very gently for 20—30 minutes, until the salmon is cooked. Transfer the fish to a warm serving dish and keep hot.

Liquidize the vegetables and stock, or pass them through a sieve. Beat the egg yolks well, add the stock gradually, beating all the time to prevent curdling. Return to the pan and reheat until almost boiling, but do not allow the sauce to boil. Season the sauce to taste and pour over the salmon. Serve garnished with thinly sliced cucumber and parsley.

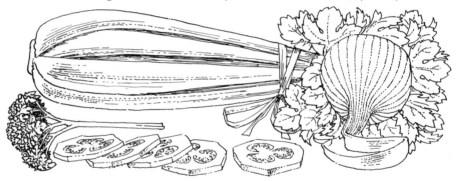

Haddock bonne femme

Serves 2
310 calories per serving

Imperial	Metric	American
2 small onions	2 small onions	2 small onions
2 oz. mushrooms	50 g. mushrooms	½ cup mushrooms
4 teaspoons chopped parsley	4 teaspoons chopped parsley	4 teaspoons chopped parsley
seasoning	seasoning	seasoning
12 oz. filleted haddock	350 g. filleted haddock	¾ lb. filleted haddock
juice 1 lemon	juice 1 lemon	juice 1 lemon
½ pint stock	3 decilitres stock	1¼ cups stock
1 oz. butter	25 g. butter	2 tablespoons butter

Chop the onions finely. Slice the mushrooms. Grease an ovenproof dish and sprinkle with half the onions, parsley and mushrooms. Place the seasoned fillets of fish on the vegetables and place the remaining vegetables on top. Sprinkle with half the lemon juice and add the stock. Cover with greased paper and bake in a moderately hot oven (375°F., 190°C., Gas Mark 5) for 20 minutes.

Remove the fish to a warmed serving dish to. keep warm. Pour the juices into a small pan and boil until reduced in volume by half. Remove from the heat and work the butter in gradually, then stir vigorously until the sauce thickens. Season, add the lemon juice and pour over the fish.

Stuffed whiting fillets

Serves 2
206 calories per serving

Imperial	Metric	American
2 (4 oz.) smoked whiting fillets	2 (100 g.) smoked whiting fillets	2 (4 oz.) smoked whiting fillets
¼ pint milk	1½ decilitres milk	⅔ cup milk
for the stuffing:	**for the stuffing:**	**for the stuffing:**
3 oz. mushrooms	75 g. mushrooms	¾ cup mushrooms
1 small onion	1 small onion	1 small onion
salt	salt	salt
ground black pepper	ground black pepper	ground black pepper
1 tablespoon chopped parsley	1 tablespoon chopped parsley	1 tablespoon chopped parsley
1 large cooking apple	1 large cooking apple	1 large baking apple

Cut each fillet in half lengthways. Chop the mushrooms and mix with the finely chopped onion, seasoning, parsley and peeled, cored and coarsely chopped apple. Spread the stuffing on the fish fillets. Roll up from the head towards the tail. Place together in a casserole and add the milk.

Cover the casserole and cook in a moderate oven (350°F., 180°C., Gas Mark 4) for 15–20 minutes. Drain and serve immediately.

Liver casserole

Serves 2
343 calories per serving

Imperial	Metric	American
4 rashers lean bacon	4 rashers lean bacon	4 lean bacon slices
4 oz. lambs' liver	100 g. lambs' liver	¼ lb. lamb liver
4 oz. mushrooms	100 g. mushrooms	1 cup mushrooms
1 medium onion	1 medium onion	1 medium onion
2 tomatoes	2 tomatoes	2 tomatoes
seasoning	seasoning	seasoning

Cut two pieces of aluminium foil and place two rashers of bacon in the middle of each piece. Place half the liver on top of the bacon and cover with sliced mushrooms, sliced onion, sliced tomato and seasoning. Carefully pinch the edges of the foil into a paper bag shape, so that the juices cannot escape. Put the parcels on a baking tin on the highest shelf of the oven (375°F., 190°C., Gas Mark 5) for about ½ hour. Serve hot with the meat juices and green vegetables.

Steak and mushroom bake

Serves 2
573 calories per serving

Imperial	Metric	American
12 oz. best lean stewing steak	350 g. best lean stewing steak	¾ lb. best lean beef stewmeat
½ beef stock cube	½ beef stock cube	½ beef bouillon cube
½ pint tomato juice	3 decilitres tomato juice	1¼ cups tomato juice
salt and pepper	salt and pepper	salt and pepper
6 oz. mushrooms	175 g. mushrooms	1½ cups mushrooms
2 oz. soft white bread-crumbs	50 g. soft white bread-crumbs	1 cup soft white bread crumbs

Cut the steak into bite-sized pieces and put into a pan with the stock cube, dissolved in a little boiling water. Reserve about a third of the tomato juice and add the rest to the meat, season. Bring to the boil, cover and simmer very gently for about 1½ hours.

Add the remaining tomato juice and the mushrooms and simmer for another 30 minutes. Place in a casserole, sprinkle with breadcrumbs and brown under the grill until the crumbs are golden brown.

Cheese omelette (page 42)

Summer lamb casserole

Serves 2
400 calories per serving

Imperial	Metric	American
8 oz. cooked, lean leg lamb	225 g. cooked, lean leg lamb	½ lb. cooked, lean leg lamb
½ onion	½ onion	½ onion
½ tablespoon oil	½ tablespoon oil	½ tablespoon oil
½ small can tomatoes	½ small can tomatoes	½ small can tomatoes
3½ tablespoons chicken stock	3½ tablespoons chicken stock	¼ cup chicken stock
½ tablespoon tomato purée	½ tablespoon tomato purée	½ tablespoon tomato paste
2 whole new carrots	2 whole new carrots	2 whole new carrots
bouquet garni	bouquet garni	bouquet garni
salt and pepper	salt and pepper	salt and pepper
2 oz. peas	50 g. peas	generous ⅓ cup peas
2 oz. whole French beans	50 g. whole French beans	4 French beans
to garnish:	**to garnish:**	**to garnish:**
parsley	parsley	parsley

Cut the lamb into 1-inch (2½-cm.) cubes and trim off all excess fat. Sauté the chopped onion in the oil. Add the meat, tomatoes, stock, purée, carrots, bouquet garni and seasoning. Bring to the boil and simmer for 20 minutes. Add the peas and beans and simmer for a further 10 minutes. Remove the bouquet garni, adjust the seasoning and garnish before serving.

Murtoa barbecued kidneys in wine sauce

Serves 2
462 calories per serving

Imperial	Metric	American
6 lambs' kidneys	6 lambs' kidneys	6 lamb kidneys
1 oz. butter	25 g. butter	2 tablespoons butter
½ large onion	½ large onion	½ large onion
scant ½ oz. flour	scant 15 g. flour	scant 2 tablespoons flour
4 tablespoons water	4 tablespoons water	⅓ cup water
½ beef stock cube	½ beef stock cube	½ beef bouillon cube
¼ pint red wine	1½ decilitres red wine	⅔ cup red wine
little garlic salt	little garlic salt	little garlic salt
1 small bay leaf	1 small bay leaf	1 small bay leaf
1 oz. mushrooms	25 g. mushrooms	¼ cup mushrooms
salt and pepper	salt and pepper	salt and pepper
½ tablespoon chopped parsley	½ tablespoon chopped parsley	½ tablespoon chopped parsley

Wash the kidneys thoroughly and dry. Remove the skin and fat and cut down lengthways without separating the two halves. Remove the cores. Skewer the kidneys and brush over with a little melted butter. Grill until just cooked—about 4–5 minutes on each side.

Meanwhile, melt the remaining butter in a pan and fry the finely chopped onion slowly until soft and light brown. Add the flour, water, stock cube and red wine, blending well until smooth. Then add the garlic salt, bay leaf, thinly sliced mushrooms and salt and pepper to taste. Bring to the boil, stirring all the time and simmer until the sauce thickens. Remove the bay leaf.

Arrange the cooked kidneys on a serving dish and pour the wine sauce over. Sprinkle with chopped parsley. This dish could be served with a green salad.

Summer beef roll

Serves 2
495 calories per serving

Imperial	Metric	American
½ (4 oz.) packet sage and onion stuffing	½ (100 g.) packet sage and onion stuffing	½ (4 oz.) package sage and onion or savory stuffing mix
6 oz. raw minced beef	175 g. raw minced beef	¾ cup firmly packed raw ground beef
2 oz. streaky bacon	50 g. streaky bacon	3 bacon slices
1 very small onion	1 very small onion	1 very small onion
½ teaspoon made mustard	½ teaspoon made mustard	½ teaspoon prepared mustard
salt and pepper	salt and pepper	salt and pepper
1 egg, beaten	1 egg, beaten	1 egg, beaten
golden breadcrumbs	golden breadcrumbs	golden, dried bread crumbs

Prepare the stuffing as directed on the packet. Combine the stuffing with the minced beef, derinded and minced bacon, grated onion and mustard. Season with salt and pepper. Shape the mixture into a roll, brush with beaten egg and coat with golden crumbs.

Place on a roasting tray and bake in a moderate oven (350°F., 180°C., Gas Mark 4) for 1 hour or until cooked. Cut in slices. Serve cold with salad.

Chicken and ham filled green pepper

Serves 2
214 calories per serving

Imperial	Metric	American
2 large green peppers	2 large green peppers	2 large green sweet peppers
for the stuffing:	**for the stuffing:**	**for the stuffing:**
2 oz. cooked chicken, minced	50 g. cooked chicken, minced	¼ cup cooked ground chicken
2 oz. cooked ham, minced	50 g. cooked ham, minced	¼ cup cooked ground ham
1 small onion, minced	1 small onion, minced	1 small onion, ground
1 oz. mushrooms, chopped	25 g. mushrooms, chopped	¼ cup chopped mushrooms
¼ teaspoon dried marjoram	¼ teaspoon dried marjoram	¼ teaspoon dried marjoram
salt and pepper	salt and pepper	salt and pepper
for the topping:	**for the topping:**	**for the topping:**
½ egg	½ egg	½ egg
½ (5 oz.) carton natural yogurt	½ (150 g.) carton natural yogurt	½ (5 oz.) carton natural yogurt
little made mustard	little made mustard	little prepared mustard
to garnish:	**to garnish:**	**to garnish:**
parsley sprigs	parsley sprigs	parsley sprigs

Cut off the stalk end of each pepper and remove the core and seeds. Blanch by placing in boiling water for 10 minutes, drain and cool under running cold water.

Combine all the ingredients for the stuffing and season. Divide between the peppers and press down well. Place in an ovenproof dish and cook in the oven (375°F., 190°C., Gas Mark 5) for 45 minutes.

Beat together the egg, yogurt and mustard and spoon a layer of this mixture on to each pepper. Cook for a further 20 minutes until the topping is set. Serve hot, garnished with parsley sprigs.

Rabbit casserole

Serves 2
338 calories per serving

Imperial	Metric	American
4 (2 oz.) pieces boneless rabbit	4 (50 g.) pieces boneless rabbit	4 (2 oz.) pieces boneless rabbit
$\frac{1}{4}$ tablespoon oil	$\frac{1}{4}$ tablespoon oil	$\frac{1}{4}$ tablespoon oil
$\frac{1}{2}$ tablespoon butter	$\frac{1}{2}$ tablespoon butter	$\frac{1}{2}$ tablespoon butter
1 small onion	1 small onion	1 small onion
1 small wine glass red wine	1 small wine glass red wine	1 small wine glass red wine
$\frac{1}{4}$ pint hot water	$1\frac{1}{2}$ decilitres hot water	$\frac{2}{3}$ cup hot water
pinch pepper	pinch pepper	dash pepper
1 tablespoon chopped capers	1 tablespoon chopped capers	1 tablespoon chopped capers
1 oz. tomato purée	25 g. tomato purée	2 tablespoons tomato paste
$\frac{1}{2}$ chicken stock cube	$\frac{1}{2}$ chicken stock cube	$\frac{1}{2}$ chicken bouillon cube
$\frac{1}{2}$ teaspoon salt	$\frac{1}{2}$ teaspoon salt	$\frac{1}{2}$ teaspoon salt
1 stick celery, chopped	1 stick celery, chopped	1 stalk celery, chopped
1 tablespoon cornflour	1 tablespoon cornflour	1 tablespoon cornstarch

Place the rabbit in a casserole. Heat oil and butter in a frying pan and fry the chopped onion until brown. Add to the rabbit with the remaining ingredients, except the cornflour. Cover and cook in a moderate oven (350°F., 180°C., Gas Mark 4) for about $1\frac{1}{2}$ hours.

If a thickened sauce is preferred, blend the cornflour with a little cold water and add to the casserole. Allow to cook for a few more minutes.

Stuffed courgettes

Serves 2
227 calories per serving

Imperial	Metric	American
2 medium courgettes	2 medium courgettes	2 medium small zucchini
2 tomatoes	2 tomatoes	2 tomatoes
1 oz. butter or margarine	25 g. butter or margarine	2 tablespoons butter or margarine
$\frac{1}{2}$ onion	$\frac{1}{2}$ onion	$\frac{1}{2}$ onion
little paprika pepper	little paprika pepper	little paprika pepper
salt and pepper	salt and pepper	salt and pepper
4 oz. prawns	100 g. prawns	$\frac{2}{3}$ cup prawns or shrimp
little Parmesan cheese	little Parmesan cheese	little Parmesan cheese

Trim off each end of the courgettes. Cook whole for about 5 minutes in boiling salted water. Drain and run cold water over them for a few seconds, to preserve the colour.

Remove a thin slice lengthways from the courgettes. Carefully scoop out the flesh with a teaspoon and chop. Skin the tomatoes, discard the seeds and chop roughly. Put the butter into a saucepan and add the chopped onion; cook until soft but not brown. Add the paprika, chopped courgette flesh and tomatoes. Season and cook for 3 minutes. Stir in the prawns.

Put the courgette cases in a buttered gratin dish and fill them with the mixture. Dust with Parmesan cheese and brown in a hot oven (425°F., 220°C., Gas Mark 7) for about 15 minutes.

Barbecued seafood skewers (page 61)

Desserts

Apple whip

Serves 2
132 calories per serving

Imperial	Metric	American
8 oz. cooking apples	225 g. cooking apples	½ lb. baking apples
flesh and juice 1 orange	flesh and juice 1 orange	flesh and juice 1 orange
2 drops liquid artificial sweetener, if liked	2 drops liquid artificial sweetener, if liked	2 drops liquid artificial sweetener, if liked
1 egg, separated	1 egg, separated	1 egg, separated
1 red-skinned apple	1 red-skinned apple	1 red-skinned apple

Simmer the peeled, cored and sliced apples, orange flesh and juice with artificial sweetener, until the fruit is tender. Beat to a purée and stir in the egg yolk. Chill. Fold in the stiffly beaten egg white.

Arrange the apple whip and red-skinned apple slices in alternate layers in stemmed glasses, finishing with a layer of whip. Serve very cold.

Pear and strawberry mould

Serves 2
136 calories per serving

Imperial	Metric	American
½ pint water	3 decilitres water	1¼ cups water
grated rind 1 lemon	grated rind 1 lemon	grated rind 1 lemon
juice 2 lemons	juice 2 lemons	juice 2 lemons
¾ tablespoon gelatine	¾ tablespoon gelatine	1 tablespoon gelatin
artificial sweetener to taste	artificial sweetener to taste	artificial sweetener to taste
drop vanilla essence	drop vanilla essence	drop vanilla extract
2 tablespoons milk powder	2 tablespoons milk powder	3 tablespoons milk powder
2 ripe pears	2 ripe pears	2 ripe pears
6 oz. strawberries	175 g. strawberries	generous 1 cup strawberries

Place the water, rind and juice of the lemons in a pan. Bring to the boil and remove from the heat. Cool. Dissolve the gelatine in a little water and add to the pan with the lemon. Pour into a bowl and allow to become cold. Whisk in the artificial sweetener, vanilla essence and milk powder. Chill until beginning to set. Whisk the mixture until thick and foamy, add the peeled, cored and chopped pears and hulled and halved strawberries. Pour into a mould and allow to set. Unmould on to a dish and serve.

Apricot mousse

Serves 2
150 calories per serving

Imperial	Metric	American
4 oz. dried apricots	100 g. dried apricots	¾ cup dried apricots
rind and juice 1 large lemon	rind and juice 1 large lemon	rind and juice 1 large lemon
artificial sweetener to taste	artificial sweetener to taste	artificial sweetener to taste
2 egg whites	2 egg whites	2 egg whites
to decorate:	**to decorate:**	**to decorate:**
few toasted flaked almonds	few toasted flaked almonds	few toasted flaked almonds

Soak the apricots overnight in water. Poach them in just enough water to cover for about 20 minutes, or until tender. Add the finely grated rind and juice of the lemon and artificial sweetener to taste. Cook for a further 10 minutes, stirring from time to time. Rub through a sieve or blend in a liquidizer to a purée. Allow to cool. Whisk the egg whites until stiff and fold into the purée. Turn into glasses and chill before serving. Decorate with flaked almonds.

Entertaining

Nowadays, when so many people are weight conscious, it is best to plan your dinner parties on the assumption that maybe half your guests will be on a diet.

This does not mean that you cannot add those little extra touches to your cooking, which makes entertaining such fun. But it does mean that you have to plan your meals that little bit more carefully. Some of your guests, like yourself, will probably have cut down on their calorie intake on or before the day they are dining with you, so that the odd spoonful of cream will not be a disaster.

It is much better to have a low-calorie starter, a rich main course, when you can really let yourself go, and then either fresh fruit or a low-calorie dessert. Please do not try to force second helpings on your guests, either. We have all suffered from the hostess who kept insisting that we should have just one more potato or another soupçon of sauce. It is always difficult to refuse these without giving offence. So when your diet conscious guests say 'enough', accept that they mean it.

Dieting, like everything else, has to be treated with a sense of proportion. You invite your friends to dine with you so that you can enjoy their company, and this means calorie counting the meal in advance. Then, when you sit down to the table, no-one needs to worry about their waistline, least of all you. You can all concentrate on enjoying the food, wine and conversation.

I have also included some suggestions for a slimmers' buffet party.

Starters

Dorset scalloped crab

Serves 4
79 calories per serving

Imperial	Metric	American
1 good-sized crab (about 1½ lb.)	1 good-sized crab (about 700 g.)	1 good-sized crab (about 1½ lb.)
1 anchovy, chopped	1 anchovy, chopped	1 anchovy, chopped
2 tablespoons soft bread-crumbs	2 tablespoons soft bread-crumbs	3 tablespoons soft bread crumbs
2 tablespoons vinegar	2 tablespoons vinegar	3 tablespoons vinegar
½ oz. butter	15 g. butter	1 tablespoon butter
salt	salt	salt
cayenne pepper	cayenne pepper	cayenne pepper
to garnish:	**to garnish:**	**to garnish:**
parsley	parsley	parsley

Remove the crab meat from the body of the shell and mix with the rest of the ingredients. Put all the ingredients into a saucepan and simmer gently until well mixed. Heap lightly into four scallop shells. Place in a moderate oven till lightly browned and garnish with parsley. Serve at once.

Citrus salad in buttermilk dressing

Serves 4
67 calories per serving

Imperial	Metric	American
2 oranges	2 oranges	2 oranges
1 grapefruit	1 grapefruit	1 grapefruit
2 tablespoons finely chopped fresh mint	2 tablespoons finely chopped fresh mint	3 tablespoons finely chopped fresh mint
$\frac{1}{2}$ pint buttermilk	3 decilitres buttermilk	$1\frac{1}{4}$ cups buttermilk
to garnish:	**to garnish:**	**to garnish:**
sprigs mint	sprigs mint	sprigs mint

Grate the zest from 1 orange. Place in a bowl. Remove all the peel and pith from the oranges and grapefruit and discard. Then, over the bowl, carefully cut between the membranes to remove the fruit segments. Add the chopped mint and buttermilk to the grated zest and fruit segments in the bowl. Mix well. Leave in the refrigerator to marinate for about 1 hour. Spoon into individual glass dishes. Garnish with the sprigs of mint.

Cream of asparagus soup

Serves 4
55 calories per serving

Imperial	Metric	American
1 medium onion	1 medium onion	1 medium onion
$1\frac{1}{4}$ pints chicken stock	$\frac{3}{4}$ litre chicken stock	generous 3 cups chicken stock
1 (12 oz.) can asparagus spears	1 (350 g.) can asparagus spears	1 (12 oz.) can asparagus spears
salt and pepper	salt and pepper	salt and pepper
4 tablespoons single cream	4 tablespoons single cream	$\frac{1}{3}$ cup coffee cream

Peel and slice the onion and simmer it in the chicken stock until tender. Drain the asparagus and add the liquor to the pan. Season to taste. Chop the asparagus, leaving a few tips for garnish. Add to the pan and simmer for 10 minutes. Sieve well.

Reheat if necessary and just before serving add a tablespoon of cream to each portion.

Smoked haddock and yogurt mousse

Serves 4
140 calories per serving

Imperial	Metric	American
1 ($7\frac{1}{2}$ oz.) packet frozen, cook-in-the-bag smoked haddock fillets	1 (215 g.) packet frozen, cook-in-the-bag smoked haddock fillets	1 ($7\frac{1}{2}$ oz.) package frozen, cook-in-the-bag smoked haddock fillets
2 (5 oz.) cartons natural yogurt	2 (150 g.) cartons natural yogurt	2 (5 oz.) cartons natural yogurt
2 hard-boiled eggs	2 hard-boiled eggs	2 hard-cooked eggs
small bunch watercress	small bunch watercress	small bunch watercress
grated zest $\frac{1}{2}$ lemon	grated zest $\frac{1}{2}$ lemon	grated zest $\frac{1}{2}$ lemon
2 teaspoons gelatine	2 teaspoons gelatine	2 teaspoons gelatin
2 teaspoons lemon juice	2 teaspoons lemon juice	2 teaspoons lemon juice
2 tablespoons water	2 tablespoons water	3 tablespoons water
salt and pepper	salt and pepper	salt and pepper

Cook the smoked haddock according to instructions. Remove from the cooking bag and reserve the liquor. Skin and flake the fish finely. Mix with the yogurt and one chopped hard-boiled egg. Chop all but a few sprigs of watercress and add to the fish mixture with the grated lemon zest.

In a bowl over hot water, dissolve the gelatine in the lemon juice, water and fish liquor and fold into the fish mixture. Season well and spoon into four individual dishes or one larger dish. Chill until set. Garnish with sprigs of watercress and the remaining hard-boiled egg, sliced.

Slimmers' 'open sandwiches' (page 69)

Lemon and tuna baskets

Serves 6
75 calories per serving

Imperial	Metric	American
3 large lemons	3 large lemons	3 large lemons
1 (7 oz.) can tuna fish	1 (200 g.) can tuna fish	1 (7 oz.) can tuna fish
3 tablespoons dry white wine	3 tablespoons dry white wine	scant ¼ cup dry white wine
2 tablespoons chopped chives	2 tablespoons chopped chives	3 tablespoons chopped chives
salt	salt	salt
freshly ground black pepper	freshly ground black pepper	freshly ground black pepper
2 tablespoons soured cream	2 tablespoons soured cream	3 tablespoons sour cream
to garnish:	**to garnish:**	**to garnish:**
few capers	few capers	few capers

Cut the lemons in half lengthways and scoop out the flesh. Strain off the juice. Blend the drained tuna fish, lemon juice and wine together. Add the chives, seasoning and lastly fold in the soured cream. Pile back into the lemon shells and garnish with capers.

Mushrooms à la greque

This is a French provincial first course, which most people find very enjoyable.
Serves 4
136 calories per serving

Imperial	Metric	American
8 oz. button mushrooms	225 g. button mushrooms	2 cups button mushrooms
3–4 tablespoons olive oil	3–4 tablespoons olive oil	4–5 tablespoons olive oil
3–4 tablespoons vinegar	3–4 tablespoons vinegar	4–5 tablespoons vinegar
salt and pepper	salt and pepper	salt and pepper
French mustard	French mustard	French mustard
liquid artificial sweetener	liquid artificial sweetener	liquid artificial sweetener
chopped parsley	chopped parsley	chopped parsley

Wash the mushrooms. If they are very small, leave them whole, otherwise slice them. Mix the olive oil and vinegar with seasonings and a drop or two of artificial sweetener to taste. Toss the mushrooms in the dressing and leave to stand for at least an hour before serving. Sprinkle with a little chopped parsley.

Tomato jelly

This is a delicious starter, made with canned tomatoes. It can be served on its own, or garnished with a few prawns or slices of cucumber.
Serves 4
30 calories per serving

Imperial	Metric	American
1 (16 oz.) can tomatoes	1 (450 g.) can tomatoes	1 (16 oz.) can tomatoes
salt and pepper	salt and pepper	salt and pepper
celery salt	celery salt	celery salt
Worcestershire sauce	Worcestershire sauce	Worcestershire sauce
liquid artificial sweetener	liquid artificial sweetener	liquid artificial sweetener
1 tablespoon gelatine	1 tablespoon gelatine	1 tablespoon gelatin
2 tablespoons boiling water	2 tablespoons boiling water	3 tablespoons boiling water

Purée the tomatoes by passing them through a sieve at least twice. Add the seasonings and a drop of artificial sweetener. Dissolve the gelatine in the boiling water and mix in with the tomatoes. Pour into a mould and allow to set. Serve garnished as suggested.

Main dishes

Barbecued seafood skewers

Illustrated in colour on page 55
Serves 4
150 calories per serving

Imperial	Metric	American
for the baste:	**for the baste:**	**for the baste:**
grated rind and juice 1 lemon	grated rind and juice 1 lemon	grated rind and juice 1 lemon
2 tablespoons tomato purée	2 tablespoons tomato purée	3 tablespoons tomato paste
1 teaspoon Worcestershire sauce	1 teaspoon Worcestershire sauce	1 teaspoon Worcestershire sauce
$\frac{1}{4}$ teaspoon salt	$\frac{1}{4}$ teaspoon salt	$\frac{1}{4}$ teaspoon salt
ground black pepper	ground black pepper	ground black pepper
1 clove garlic, crushed	1 clove garlic, crushed	1 clove garlic, crushed
for the skewers:	**for the skewers:**	**for the skewers:**
3 rashers back bacon	3 rashers back bacon	3 lean bacon slices
1 ($7\frac{1}{2}$ oz.) packet frozen plaice fillets	1 (215 g.) packet frozen plaice fillets	1 ($7\frac{1}{2}$ oz.) package frozen sole fillets
4 Dublin Bay prawns or 2 crayfish tails	4 Dublin Bay prawns or 2 crayfish tails	4 jumbo-size shrimp or 2 crayfish tails
1 large lemon	1 large lemon	1 large lemon
16 cooked, peeled prawns	16 cooked, peeled prawns	16 cooked, peeled prawns or shrimp
for the sauce:	**for the sauce:**	**for the sauce:**
1 (5 oz.) carton natural yogurt	1 (150 g.) carton natural yogurt	1 (5 oz.) carton natural yogurt
1 tablespoon tomato purée	1 tablespoon tomato purée	1 tablespoon tomato paste
1 teaspoon lemon juice	1 teaspoon lemon juice	1 teaspoon lemon juice
$\frac{1}{2}$ teaspoon lemon rind	$\frac{1}{2}$ teaspoon lemon rind	$\frac{1}{2}$ teaspoon lemon rind
1 teaspoon Worcestershire sauce	1 teaspoon Worcestershire sauce	1 teaspoon Worcestershire sauce
$\frac{1}{2}$ teaspoon grated or finely chopped onion	$\frac{1}{2}$ teaspoon grated or finely chopped onion	$\frac{1}{2}$ teaspoon grated or finely chopped onion
2 teaspoons chopped parsley	2 teaspoons chopped parsley	2 teaspoons chopped parsley
salt and pepper	salt and pepper	salt and pepper

Reserving $\frac{1}{2}$ teaspoon of grated rind and 1 teaspoon lemon juice for the sauce, whisk all the remaining ingredients for the baste together. Remove the rind and any fat from the bacon rashers and place them on a board. Stretch with the back of a round-bladed knife. Cut each in four. Remove the skin from the thawed plaice fillets and divide into 12 pieces. Place each piece on a rasher of bacon, season and roll up, en-closing the fish. Halve the peeled Dublin Bay prawns, or cut the peeled crayfish tails into 4 equal pieces. Cut the lemon into 4 thick slices and then cut each lemon slice into 4 pieces.

Divide the seafood between 4 long or 8 shorter skewers, alternating with pieces of lemon.

Brush the seafood with the baste. Place the skewers on a barbecue for 8–10 minutes until the fish is cooked, turning and brushing occasionally with the baste.

Alternatively, place under a moderate grill for 10–12 minutes, turning and brushing with the baste.

Stir all the ingredients for the sauce together, using the reserved lemon rind and juice. Season to taste.

Seafood curry

Serves 4
245 calories per serving

Imperial	Metric	American
1 lb. sole fillets	450 g. sole fillets	1 lb. sole fillets
juice ½ lemon	juice ½ lemon	juice ½ lemon
1 oz. margarine	25 g. margarine	2 tablespoons margarine
1 tablespoon curry powder	1 tablespoon curry powder	1 tablespoon curry powder
2 teaspoons grated lemon rind	2 teaspoons grated lemon rind	2 teaspoons grated lemon rind
2 teaspoons flour	2 teaspoons flour	2 teaspoons flour
¼ pint fish stock	1½ decilitres fish stock	⅔ cup fish stock
½ pint light stock	3 decilitres light stock	1¼ cups light stock
seasoning	seasoning	seasoning
1½ oz. sultanas	65 g. sultanas	⅓ cup seedless white raisins
2 apples	2 apples	2 apples
4 oz. peeled prawns	100 g. peeled prawns	1⅓ cups peeled prawns
2 tomatoes	2 tomatoes	2 tomatoes

Cut the skinned sole into strips and then into cubes. Poach gently in the lemon juice and water until tender. Drain the fish but reserve the liquid. Melt the margarine and add the curry powder and lemon rind. Cook for a few minutes. Stir in the flour and cook for a further 2 minutes, then gradually add the fish juices and stock. Add the seasoning and sultanas. Simmer for 15 minutes. Add the sole, peeled, cored and sliced apples, prawns and quartered tomatoes and bring to the boil.

Serve accompanied by a little saffron rice for your guests.

Lamb moussaka with yogurt topping

Serves 4
392 calories per serving

Imperial	Metric	American
1 oz. butter	25 g. butter	2 tablespoons butter
2 cloves garlic	2 cloves garlic	2 cloves garlic
2 medium onions	2 medium onions	2 medium onions
2 aubergines	2 aubergines	2 eggplants
1 (14 oz.) can tomatoes	1 (400 g.) can tomatoes	1 (14 oz.) can tomatoes
12 oz. cooked lean lamb, minced	350 g. cooked lean lamb, minced	1½ cups cooked, lean ground lamb
½ teaspoon dried oregano	½ teaspoon dried oregano	½ teaspoon dried oregano
1 teaspoon fresh rosemary	1 teaspoon fresh rosemary	1 teaspoon fresh rosemary
salt and freshly ground black pepper	salt and freshly ground black pepper	salt and freshly ground black pepper
2 (5 oz.) cartons natural yogurt	2 (150 g.) cartons natural yogurt	2 (5 oz.) cartons natural yogurt
3 egg yolks	3 egg yolks	3 egg yolks
1 tablespoon grated Parmesan cheese	1 tablespoon grated Parmesan cheese	1 tablespoon grated Parmesan cheese

Melt the butter in a flameproof casserole, add the crushed garlic, sliced onions and blanched and sliced aubergines and cook for 10 minutes, mixing well. Add the tomatoes, meat, oregano, rosemary, salt and pepper. Cover and cook slowly for 10 minutes. Spoon the yogurt into a small saucepan, beat well. Beat the egg yolks together and add to the yogurt. Cook *very gently* until it thickens. Pour over the vegetables in the casserole. Sprinkle with Parmesan cheese.

Place on the middle shelf in a moderate oven (350°F., 180°C., Gas Mark 4) for 30 minutes.

Slimmers' party punch (page 72)

Veal with orange

Serves 4
375 calories per serving

Imperial	Metric	American
1¼ lb. boned loin veal	600 g. boned loin veal	1¼ lb. boned loin veal
1 oz. butter	25 g. butter	2 tablespoons butter
salt and pepper	salt and pepper	salt and pepper
few drops liquid artificial sweetener	few drops liquid artificial sweetener	few drops liquid artificial sweetener
3 carrots	3 carrots	3 carrots
2 oranges	2 oranges	2 oranges
¼ pint white stock	1½ decilitres white stock	⅔ cup white stock
2 tablespoons lemon juice	2 tablespoons lemon juice	3 tablespoons lemon juice

Cut the veal into strips 1 × 3 inches (2½ × 7½ cm.) long, removing any fat. Sauté the meat in the butter until browned. Remove from the pan and drain well. Place the meat in a casserole dish, sprinkle with seasoning and artificial sweetener, if liked. Place the thinly sliced carrots and peeled and sliced oranges on top. Pour the stock and lemon juice over and bake in a moderate oven (350°F., 180°C., Gas Mark 4) for 45 minutes or until the meat is tender. Uncover and bake for 10 minutes longer. Adjust the seasoning and serve.

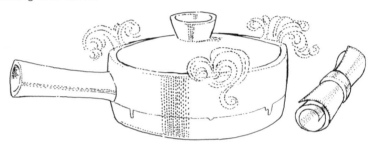

Pork paprika

Serves 4
395 calories per serving

Imperial	Metric	American
salt and pepper	salt and pepper	salt and pepper
4 lean boneless pork chops	4 lean boneless pork chops	4 lean boneless pork chops
1 onion	1 onion	1 onion
½ tablespoon oil	½ tablespoon oil	½ tablespoon oil
paprika pepper	paprika pepper	paprika pepper
1 (2½ oz.) can tomato purée	1 (65 g.) can tomato purée	1 (2½ oz.) can tomato paste
¼ pint stock	1½ decilitres stock	⅔ cup stock
6 oz. button mushrooms	175 g. button mushrooms	1½ cups button mushrooms
2 (5 oz.) cartons natural yogurt	2 (150 g.) cartons natural yogurt	2 (5 oz.) cartons natural yogurt

Season the pork chops and put under the grill to 'seal' on both sides. Remove from the heat and cut off any fat. Keep to one side. In a casserole, gently cook the chopped onion in the oil until soft. Blend in the paprika pepper and cook for a further minute. Add the tomato purée. Remove from the heat and blend in the stock. Return to the heat and bring to the boil, stirring well. Taste and adjust seasoning. Add the pork chops.

Cover and cook in a moderate oven (350°F., 180°C., Gas Mark 4), for 1–1¼ hours until the meat is tender. Five minutes before the end of the cooking time add the mushrooms. Spoon over the yogurt just before serving.

Spiced veal and bacon rolls

Serves 4
429 calories per serving (without wine)
459 calories per serving (with wine)

Imperial	Metric	American
12 oz. veal fillet	350 g. veal fillet	¾ lb. veal round
6 oz. shortback bacon rashers	175 g. shortback bacon rashers	6 oz. lean bacon slices
about 1 tablespoon made mustard	about 1 tablespoon made mustard	about 1 tablespoon prepared mustard
salt and pepper	salt and pepper	salt and pepper
2 tablespoons salad oil	2 tablespoons salad oil	3 tablespoons salad oil
1 oz. butter	25 g. butter	2 tablespoons butter
2 medium onions	2 medium onions	2 medium onions
1 clove garlic (optional)	1 clove garlic (optional)	1 clove garlic (optional)
1 oz. flour	25 g. flour	¼ cup flour
½ pint water	3 decilitres water	1¼ cups water
1 chicken stock cube	1 chicken stock cube	1 chicken bouillon cube
¼ pint white wine or water	1½ decilitres white wine or water	⅔ cup white wine or water
1 tablespoon tomato purée	1 tablespoon tomato purée	1 tablespoon tomato paste
¼ teaspoon dried herbs	¼ teaspoon dried herbs	¼ teaspoon dried herbs

Ask your butcher to thinly slice and flatten the veal. Trim the veal into pieces about 2 × 1½ inches (5 × 3½ cm.). Cut the rind off the bacon and stretch the bacon out with the back of a knife on a wooden board; cut into 2-inch (5-cm.) lengths. Spread each piece of veal with mustard and season lightly with salt and pepper. Roll up with a piece of bacon around the outside and secure with a wooden cocktail stick.

Heat the oil in a pan, add the butter and quickly brown the veal and bacon rolls, then lift them into an ovenproof casserole. Peel the onions and cut into wedges, fry these in the pan until pale brown and lift into the casserole. Add the crushed garlic. Stir the flour into the remaining fat to make a roux, adding a little more butter if necessary to make it smooth. Remove from the heat and add the water slowly, then the crumbled stock cube, wine or extra water, tomato purée and dried herbs. Return to the heat and bring to the boil. Season to taste, then pour over the veal rolls. Cover with a lid and simmer in a moderate oven (325°F., 170°C., Gas Mark 3) for 1 hour. Serve hot with a tossed green salad or with new potatoes and green peas for guests.

Turkey and fruit salad

Christmas is THE time for entertaining, but sometimes you get a bit tired of the same old roast turkey, followed by cold turkey. So try this recipe for an exciting change.
Serves 4
357 calories per serving

Imperial	Metric	American
1 lb. cooked turkey	450 g. cooked turkey	1 lb. cooked turkey
8 oz. green grapes	225 g. green grapes	½ lb. white grapes
4 sticks celery	4 sticks celery	4 stalks celery
2 oranges	2 oranges	2 oranges
1 oz. toasted almonds	25 g. toasted almonds	¼ cup toasted almonds
1 bunch watercress	1 bunch watercress	1 bunch watercress
2 tablespoons cider vinegar	2 tablespoons cider vinegar	3 tablespoons cider vinegar
seasoning	seasoning	seasoning
pinch mustard powder	pinch mustard powder	dash mustard powder

Cut the turkey into dice and toss lightly in a bowl with the seeded grapes, chopped celery, orange segments, toasted almonds and watercress. Blend the cider vinegar, seasoning and mustard powder together. Pour over the turkey mixture and serve immediately.

Pork with spicy orange sauce

Serves 4
520 calories per serving

Imperial	Metric	American
1 oz. butter	25 g. butter	2 tablespoons butter
1 medium onion	1 medium onion	1 medium onion
1 green pepper	1 green pepper	1 green sweet pepper
1¼ lb. pork fillet, cut into 1-inch cubes	600 g. pork fillet, cut into 2½-cm. cubes	1¼ lb. pork tenderloin, cut into 1-inch cubes
½ oz. seasoned flour	15 g. seasoned flour	2 tablespoons seasoned flour
juice 2 oranges	juice 2 oranges	juice 2 oranges
grated rind ½ orange	grated rind ½ orange	grated rind ½ orange
1 tablespoon Worcestershire sauce	1 tablespoon Worcestershire sauce	1 tablespoon Worcestershire sauce
¼ pint stock	1½ decilitres stock	⅔ cup stock
salt and pepper	salt and pepper	salt and pepper
1 orange	1 orange	1 orange

Melt the butter in a pan and fry the chopped onion and pepper, which has been deseeded, blanched and cut into strips, for 3 minutes. Toss the pork in seasoned flour, add to the pan and cook for 5 minutes, turning frequently. Stir in the orange juice, grated rind, Worcestershire sauce and stock. Season. Bring to the boil and simmer for 10 minutes, stirring occasionally. With a sharp knife, cut the pith and peel completely from the orange, then cut down each side of the membrane to remove the segments. Check the seasoning and stir in the orange segments before serving.

Desserts

Slimmers' strawberry cheesecake

Serves 4
131 calories per serving

Imperial	Metric	American
1 (8 oz.) carton cottage cheese	1 (225 g.) carton cottage cheese	1 cup cottage cheese
1 (5 oz.) carton natural yogurt	1 (150 g.) carton natural yogurt	1 (5 oz.) carton natural yogurt
½ oz. powdered gelatine dissolved in 4 tablespoons water	15 g. powdered gelatine dissolved in 4 tablespoons water	2 envelopes gelatin dissolved in ⅓ cup water
8 oz. frozen strawberries, liquidized or sieved	225 g. frozen strawberries, liquidized or sieved	½ lb. frozen strawberries, liquidized or sieved
artificial sweetener to taste	artificial sweetener to taste	artificial sweetener to taste
2 egg whites	2 egg whites	2 egg whites
to decorate:	**to decorate:**	**to decorate:**
few toasted split almonds	few toasted split almonds	few toasted split almonds

Line a loose-bottomed 8-inch (20-cm.) cake tin with buttered grease-proof paper. Sieve the cottage cheese into a large bowl. Combine the yogurt and dissolved gelatine and add to the cottage cheese. Add the strawberry purée and sweetener and fold in the whipped egg whites. Turn into the prepared tin and leave to set in the refrigerator. When set, unmould and serve. Decorate with almonds.

Crêpes aux pêches

Illustrated in colour on page 31
Serves 4–6
51 calories per crêpe
27 calories per filling and sauce serving

Imperial	Metric	American
4 oz. flour	100 g. flour	1 cup all-purpose flour
1 egg and 1 yolk	1 egg and 1 yolk	1 egg and 1 yolk
8 fl. oz. skimmed milk	225 millilitres skimmed milk	scant 1 cup skimmed milk
½ teaspoon salt	½ teaspoon salt	½ teaspoon salt
4 drops liquid artificial sweetener	4 drops liquid artificial sweetener	4 drops liquid artificial sweetener
corn oil	corn oil	corn oil
for the filling:	**for the filling:**	**for the filling:**
8 peaches	8 peaches	8 peaches
4 drops liquid artificial sweetener	4 drops liquid artificial sweetener	4 drops liquid artificial sweetener

Make a batter with the flour, eggs and milk. (This will make twelve 7-inch (18-cm.) pancakes.) Add the salt and liquid artificial sweetener.

For the filling, stone and peel the peaches. Chop roughly and purée, using a liquidizer or sieve. Add the liquid artificial sweetener.

To make the pancakes, heat the pan until smoking hot. Using a rubbing of corn oil for each pancake, pour in enough batter to coat the base of the pan, turn with a knife or spatula and cook quickly. Keep warm in a clean cloth. Divide the filling into fourteen. Spread each pancake to its edge and roll up. Dilute the remaining purée with very little (2 or 3 teaspoons) water and serve as a sauce.

Slimmers' coeur à la crème with loganberries

Serves 4
117 calories per serving

Imperial	Metric	American
12 oz. cottage cheese	350 g. cottage cheese	1½ cups cottage cheese
1 (5 oz.) carton natural yogurt	1 (150 g.) carton natural yogurt	1 (5 oz.) carton natural yogurt
2 teaspoons gelatine dissolved in 2 tablespoons water	2 teaspoons gelatine dissolved in 2 tablespoons water	2 teaspoons gelatin dissolved in 3 tablespoons water
fresh loganberries	fresh loganberries	fresh loganberries

Sieve the cottage cheese. Blend in the yogurt. Stir the dissolved gelatine into the cheese mixture. Spoon and press into four individual moulds. Cover with muslin held in place with an elastic band or string and stand, muslin side down, on a wire tray over a dish. Leave to drain in the refrigerator overnight.

Turn out. Serve with fresh loganberries or any soft fruit in season.

Pink pears

Serves 4
150 calories per serving

Imperial	Metric	American
4 small pears	4 small pears	4 small pears
2 wine glasses red wine	2 wine glasses red wine	2 wine glasses red wine
2 wine glasses water	2 wine glasses water	2 wine glasses water
liquid artificial sweetener	liquid artificial sweetener	liquid artificial sweetener
1 egg white	1 egg white	1 egg white
4 tablespoons double cream	4 tablespoons double cream	⅓ cup heavy cream

Peel the pears but leave the stalks on. Place the pears in a large shallow pan and poach in the red wine and water with a little artificial sweetener to taste, until tender.

To serve, fold the stiffly beaten egg white into the cream and place a spoonful on each pear. Serve either hot or well chilled.

Slimmers' buffet party recipes

Dips are ideal for 'help yourself' buffet parties. Normally you would provide savoury biscuits or crisps for guests to scoop out the dip, but for the slimmers you should provide instead thin slices of carrot, sticks of celery (well crisped) and lengthways slices of crisp cucumber.

Creamed yogurt dip

890 calories per recipe

Imperial	Metric	American
1 (5 oz.) carton natural yogurt	1 (150 g.) carton natural yogurt	1 (5 oz.) carton natural yogurt
4 oz. cream cheese	100 g. cream cheese	½ cup cream cheese
2 tablespoons very finely chopped onion	2 tablespoons very finely chopped onion	3 tablespoons very finely chopped onion
1 teaspoon paprika pepper	1 teaspoon paprika pepper	1 teaspoon paprika pepper
½ teaspoon salt	½ teaspoon salt	½ teaspoon salt
pepper	pepper	pepper

Beat the yogurt into the cream cheese. Stir in the onion and paprika. Season to taste with salt and pepper. Place in a serving bowl and chill before serving.

Cottage cheese and pineapple dip

360 calories per recipe

Imperial	Metric	American
8 oz. cottage cheese	225 g. cottage cheese	1 cup cottage cheese
4 tablespoons natural yogurt	4 tablespoons natural yogurt	⅓ cup natural yogurt
4 heaped tablespoons finely chopped pineapple	4 heaped tablespoons finely chopped pineapple	generous ⅓ cup finely chopped pineapple
salt and pepper	salt and pepper	salt and pepper

Combine the cottage cheese with the yogurt and pineapple. Season to taste. Transfer to a bowl and serve. Garnish with chopped red pepper, if liked.

Asparagus and prawn dip

230 calories per recipe

Imperial	Metric	American
4 tablespoons chopped canned asparagus	4 tablespoons chopped canned asparagus	⅓ cup chopped canned asparagus
2 oz. peeled prawns	50 g. peeled prawns	⅓ cup peeled prawns or shrimp
2 (5 oz.) cartons natural yogurt	2 (150 g.) cartons natural yogurt	2 (5 oz.) cartons natural yogurt
salt and pepper	salt and pepper	salt and pepper

Stir the asparagus and finely chopped prawns into the yogurt. Season to taste and chill. Garnish with thin slivers of gherkin, if liked.

Celery boats

150 calories per recipe

Imperial	Metric	American
4 sticks celery	4 sticks celery	4 stalks celery
4 oz. cottage cheese	100 g. cottage cheese	½ cup cottage cheese
little paprika pepper	little paprika pepper	little paprika pepper
lettuce leaves	lettuce leaves	lettuce leaves

Cut the washed celery into 1-inch (2½-cm.) lengths. Fill each with cottage cheese and sprinkle with paprika. Serve on shredded lettuce.

Slimmers' 'open sandwiches'

Illustrated in colour on page 59

Here are some more suggestions for attractive slimmers' buffet fare. Low-calorie crispbreads can be topped with:

a) cottage cheese, chopped cucumber and prawns
b) slices of tomato and Edam cheese
c) cottage cheese, orange slices and a little chopped walnut
d) flaked smoked haddock mixed with a little low-calorie margarine and lemon
e) chopped chicken, chopped mushrooms and a little apple chutney or relish

These 'open sandwiches' may be first spread thinly with a little low-calorie margarine. Garnish with parsley, watercress or crisp lettuce.

Mushroom savouries

496 calories per recipe

Imperial	Metric	American
8 large well-shaped mushrooms	8 large well-shaped mushrooms	8 large well-shaped mushrooms
4 oz. Cheddar cheese, finely grated	100 g. Cheddar cheese, finely grated	1 cup finely grated Cheddar cheese
2 tablespoons chopped parsley	2 tablespoons chopped parsley	3 tablespoons chopped parsley
little finely chopped onion	little finely chopped onion	little finely chopped onion
salt and pepper	salt and pepper	salt and pepper
pinch garlic powder	pinch garlic powder	dash garlic powder
2 teaspoons lemon juice	2 teaspoons lemon juice	2 teaspoons lemon juice

Remove the stalks from the mushrooms. Blend together the chopped stalks, cheese, parsley, onion and salt and pepper. Add the garlic powder and lemon juice. Pile this mixture into the mushroom caps and bake in a moderate oven (350°F., 180°C., Gas Mark 4) for 15 minutes. Do not overcook.

These savouries can be made in advance and reheated just before serving.

Savouries on sticks

You can add variety to a buffet table by spearing all sorts of different items on cocktail sticks. Aim for variety of both colour and texture. Some suggestions are:

a) a cube of Cheddar cheese with a black grape
b) a cube of cold cooked chicken and a cube of fresh peach
c) a cube of boiled ham with a piece of cucumber
d) a slice of cold cooked sausage with an olive
e) a cube of cheese with a pineapple chunk

You can either serve these on a plate or stuck into a marrow or cucumber.

Drinks

Drinks can be a terrible problem to the hostess, housewife and mother! You often invite a friend over for a drink or a cup of coffee, yet wonder whether you really should have another cup of coffee; after all your daily milk allowance is only half a pint!

If it's alcohol or wine, your problem intensifies, because you have an eye on the tonic water or bitter lemon along with the gin; or you're hoping to be offered a dry white wine and not a sweeter rosé. Well, take drinks into consideration, and consider the value of WATER . . . mixed into a punch or bowl! Consider, also, the low-calorie content of un-sweetened grapefruit juice as a base for a refreshing non-alcoholic drink, like the recipe for Grapefruit sparkler.

Dry cider, natural orange juice, dry sherry, all are valuable additions to the 'bar' the slimmer runs. And if you are the guest, choose a low-calorie tonic or bitter lemon, sugar-free drinks, and avoid the drinks listed as high in calories in the calorie chart!

Non-alcoholic drinks

Lemon drink

Serves 2
45 calories per drink

Imperial	Metric	American
rind and juice 2 lemons	rind and juice 2 lemons	rind and juice 2 lemons
½ pint water	3 decilitres water	1¼ cups water
artificial sweetener to taste	artificial sweetener to taste	artificial sweetener to taste
1 egg, beaten	1 egg, beaten	1 egg, beaten
soda water	soda water	soda water

Place the lemon rind, water and artificial sweetener in a saucepan and boil for 15 minutes. Cool and strain. Stir in the egg and lemon juice. Pour into glasses and top up with soda water.

Grapefruit sparkler

Serves 2
45 calories per drink

Imperial	Metric	American
½ pint unsweetened grapefruit juice	3 decilitres unsweetened grapefruit juice	1¼ cups unsweetened grapefruit juice
2 tablespoons lemon juice	2 tablespoons lemon juice	3 tablespoons lemon juice
2 drops liquid artificial sweetener	2 drops liquid artificial sweetener	2 drops liquid artificial sweetener
1 small bottle low-calorie ginger ale	1 small bottle low-calorie ginger ale	1 small bottle low-calorie ginger ale

Mix the chilled grapefruit juice, lemon juice and artificial sweetener together. Add the ginger ale and chill.

Orange velvet

Serves 2
55 calories per drink

Imperial
1 teaspoon coffee essence
2 drops liquid artificial
  sweetener
½ pint unsweetened
  orange juice

Metric
1 teaspoon coffee essence
2 drops liquid artificial
  sweetener
3 decilitres unsweetened
  orange juice

American
1 teaspoon coffee extract
2 drops liquid artificial
  sweetener
1¼ cups unsweetened
  orange juice

Mix all the ingredients together and chill before serving.

Iced coffee shake

Serves 2
95 calories per drink if
using whole milk
50 calories per drink if
using non fat milk

Imperial
½ pint milk or made up
  instant non fat milk
2 teaspoons instant coffee
4 drops liquid artificial
  sweetener

Metric
3 decilitres milk or made
  up instant non fat milk
2 teaspoons instant coffee
4 drops liquid artificial
  sweetener

American
1¼ cups milk or made up
  instant non fat milk
2 teaspoons instant coffee
4 drops liquid artificial
  sweetener

Chill the milk and then place all the ingredients in a liquidizer or blender. Turn to maximum speed for 1 minute. Serve at once.

Thirst quencher

Serves 2
8 calories per drink

Imperial
2 small bottles low-
  calorie dry ginger
½ pint made up low-
  calorie lime juice
ice cubes
1 egg white
to decorate:
cucumber slices

Metric
2 small bottles low-
  calorie dry ginger
3 decilitres made up low-
  calorie lime juice
ice cubes
1 egg white
to decorate:
cucumber slices

American
2 small bottles low-
  calorie dry ginger
1¼ cups made up low-
  calorie lime juice
ice cubes
1 egg white
to decorate:
cucumber slices

Chill the dry ginger and lime juice and combine them together. Pour on to ice cubes in tall glasses. Whisk the egg white until it stands in peaks and spoon on top of the drinks. Decorate with cucumber slices and serve at once.

Minty apple cocktail

Serves 2
137 calories per drink

Imperial
½ pint unsweetened
  apple juice
½ pint unsweetened
  orange and pineapple
  juice mixed
1 tablespoon chopped
  fresh mint
2 tablespoons water
crushed ice
to decorate:
sprigs mint

Metric
3 decilitres unsweetened
  apple juice
3 decilitres unsweetened
  orange and pineapple
  juice mixed
1 tablespoon chopped
  fresh mint
2 tablespoons water
crushed ice
to decorate:
sprigs mint

American
1¼ cups unsweetened
  apple juice
1¼ cups unsweetened
  orange and pineapple
  juice mixed
1 tablespoon chopped
  fresh mint
3 tablespoons water
crushed ice
to decorate:
sprigs mint

Combine the apple, orange and pineapple juices together. Place the mint and water in a pan. Bring to the boil. Remove from the heat and allow to infuse for 15 minutes. Strain and add the minty juice to the fruit juice. Chill well.

    Place some crushed ice in the base of two tall glasses. Pour the cocktail over and decorate with a sprig of mint.

Winter tonic

Missed lunch? This drink will keep you going until dinnertime.
Serves 1
305 calories per drink

Imperial	Metric	American
1 egg	1 egg	1 egg
1 tablespoon clear honey	1 tablespoon clear honey	1 tablespoon clear honey
1 tablespoon lemon juice	1 tablespoon lemon juice	1 tablespoon lemon juice
$\frac{1}{3}$ pint milk	$2\frac{1}{4}$ decilitres milk	generous $\frac{3}{4}$ cup milk

Separate the egg yolk and white. Whisk together the egg yolk, clear honey and lemon juice. Beat in the milk and, lastly, fold in the stiffly whisked egg white. Drink immediately.

Alcoholic drinks

Cider cup

Serves 2
77 calories per drink

Imperial	Metric	American
$\frac{1}{2}$ pint dry cider	3 decilitres dry cider	$1\frac{1}{4}$ cups cider
$\frac{1}{4}$ pint natural orange juice	$1\frac{1}{2}$ decilitres natural orange juice	$\frac{2}{3}$ cup natural orange juice
rind $\frac{1}{2}$ lemon	rind $\frac{1}{2}$ lemon	rind $\frac{1}{2}$ lemon
little ground ginger	little ground ginger	little ground ginger

Chill the cider and orange juice. Mix together then add the lemon rind and ginger. Pour into chilled glasses and decorate with slices of apple studded with cloves.

Calorie cocktail

Serves 1
150 calories per drink

Imperial	Metric	American
1 egg	1 egg	1 egg
$\frac{1}{4}$ pint unsweetened apple juice	$1\frac{1}{2}$ decilitres unsweetened apple juice	$\frac{2}{3}$ cup unsweetened apple juice
1 teaspoon dry sherry	1 teaspoon dry sherry	1 teaspoon dry sherry
ground cinnamon	ground cinnamon	ground cinnamon

Beat all the ingredients together except the cinnamon. Pour into a glass, sprinkle on a little cinnamon and serve.

Slimmers' party punch

Illustrated in colour on page 63
Serves 12
45 calories per serving

Imperial	Metric	American
1 wine glass unsweetened grape juice	1 wine glass unsweetened grape juice	1 wine glass unsweetened grape juice
2 wine glasses dry white wine	2 wine glasses dry white wine	2 wine glasses dry white wine
1 drop Angostura bitters	1 drop Angostura bitters	1 drop Angostura bitters
2 (8 fl. oz.) bottles low-calorie orange	2 (225 millilitres) bottles low-calorie orange	2 (1 cup) bottles low-calorie orange
2 (8 fl. oz.) bottles low-calorie tonic water	2 (225 millilitres) bottles low-calorie tonic water	2 (1 cup) bottles low-calorie tonic water
2 spirit measures white rum	2 spirit measures white rum	2 spirit measures white rum
1 orange	1 orange	1 orange
1 lemon	1 lemon	1 lemon
1 lime, if available	1 lime, if available	1 lime, if available
$\frac{1}{4}$ cucumber	$\frac{1}{4}$ cucumber	$\frac{1}{4}$ cucumber
sprigs mint	sprigs mint	sprigs mint

Mix all the liquids together in a punch bowl. Chill. Thinly slice the fruits and cucumber and add to the punch. Just before serving add ice cubes and a few sprigs of mint.

Sample meals

These sample meals can help you to calculate your daily calorie intake easily. Try to include a varied selection of foods over the day.

BREAKFASTS
1 glass natural orange juice
1 poached egg
1 small slice bread and butter (thinly spread)
252 calories per breakfast

1 cup coffee with milk
1 slice lean bacon
2 crispbreads with butter (thinly spread)
250 calories per breakfast

1 cup tea with milk
1 scrambled egg
1 small slice toast and butter (thinly spread)
283 calories per breakfast

1 cup coffee or tea with milk
1 slice lean bacon with grilled tomatoes
150 calories per breakfast

PACKED LUNCHES
Packed lunches can be difficult, but again the rule is to aim for variety.

1 hard-boiled egg
1 oz. (25 g.) cheese
watercress
tea with milk
1 apple
286 calories per packed lunch

2 slices lean ham (2 oz., 50 g.)
lettuce
½ tomato
few radishes
1 piece fresh fruit
1 crispbread with butter (thinly spread)
242 calories per packed lunch

LUNCHES
For the housewife at home all day, lunch should be a light meal. This means that she can eat with her family in the evening, choosing meals from this cookbook and deducting the calories already consumed during the day.

½ grapefruit
plain omelette (using 1 egg)
stewed fruit (with artificial sweetener)
178 calories per lunch

clear soup
2 oz. (50 g.) lean cold lamb with salad
1 piece fresh fruit
290 calories per lunch

tomato juice
4 oz. (100 g.) grilled liver
grilled tomato
green salad
212 calories per lunch

4 oz. (100 g.) grilled plaice
carrots
1 piece fresh fruit or junket (made with skimmed milk and artificial sweetener)
168 calories per lunch

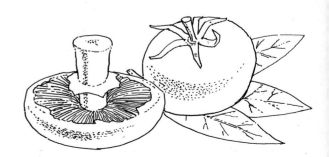

Exercises

Exercise alone is not really a good way of losing weight. You would have to do a vast amount of exercising to lose even a few pounds. But a regular daily exercise programme will give you more slender and supple lines, by toning up your muscles and firming up any flabbiness. Once you have reduced your weight by dieting, exercise will ensure that you retain your new slim lines.

So it is worth making the effort and setting aside say half an hour each day to exercise.

If you have any special health or physical problems, then check with your doctor first before you start on a programme of exercising. Remember, too, that exercises can only improve your figure if they are done regularly. There is no point in doing exercises for 30 minutes for a few days and then forgetting about them for a couple of weeks. It is usually a help if you set aside a certain time of day to do your exercises. This need not be first thing in the morning, either. Choose a time which suits you and your way of life. Don't rush things at the beginning. Start with a minute session daily and gradually work up to 30 minutes as your muscles become more supple.

Help your programme out by being more active generally. Try walking instead of waiting for a bus. Walk upstairs instead of using the lift, even walking up an escalator can help.

Be sure you are comfortably dressed when starting your exercises. No tight belts or tight sleeves. Take your shoes off.

Allow yourself half a minute relaxation between the different exercises, too, to make sure you do not become overstrained.

Exercise 1 This exercise is wonderful for toning and firming your mid-riff, waist and stomach muscles and for firming and toning the bustline.

Stand straight with your feet about 14 inches (36 cm.) apart and your hands circled loosely over your head. Breathe in deeply then bend sideways to your left as far as possible, exhaling as you go. Breathe in again as you return to your original position and exhale as you bend sideways to the right. Start off with 5 bends to each side and gradually work up to 15 bends.

Exercise 2 Swimming is marvellous for toning and firming breast and arm muscles; you can get the same effects with this form of swimming.

Stand straight, with feet together, then circle your arms backwards as if you were doing the back stroke. Both your arms should move together, but in alternate circles, i.e. when your left arm is high over your head, your right arm should be sweeping down by your thigh. Begin with 1 minute swimming and work up to 3 minutes daily.

Exercise 3 If a 'spare tyre' is your problem, this is the exercise for you.

Stand straight, feet apart, with arms out straight at shoulder level. Keeping your legs absolutely straight, swing your right arm up and then down to touch your left foot. Return to the erect position and repeat with the left arm to right foot. You may not be able to touch your feet to start with, but as you get more supple you will find it easier. Start by doing this about 5 times with each hand and work up to 15 times.

Exercise 4 This exercise also helps with midriff bulge.

Stand in the same position as for Exercise 3, but with your hands down by your sides. Slide your left hand down your left leg as if you were trying to touch your ankle. Return to the erect position and repeat with your right hand. Do this 5 times to start with and work up gradually to 10 times.

Exercise 5 This exercise helps firm your tummy muscles and your bottom.

Lie flat on your back on the floor with your arms stretched out overhead. Keeping your legs quite straight and firmly pressed to the floor, breathe in as you raise the trunk to sitting position. Breathe out as you lie back on the floor again. Do this only 3 times to start with and work up to 15 times.

Exercise 6 Lie on the floor in the same position as for Exercise 5. Breathe in deeply. Exhale as you lift your arms, head, shoulders and legs off the floor simultaneously so that your body forms a V shape. Hold this position for a few seconds. Relax and repeat 3 times.

Exercise 7 This exercise really helps to pound the inches off your hips.

Lie on the floor with your arms stretched at your sides and your palms downwards. Draw your knees up to your chest and point your toes. Then, keeping your head, shoulders and arms flat to the floor, roll your knees from side to side. Breathe in as your knees come up, and out as they move to each side. Start with 10 rolls and work up to about 20 daily.

Exercise 8 Try this one for both hips and thighs.

Sit with your back straight, arms stretched out in front of you and your legs together. Then, keeping your legs straight and your knees firm, lift each hip alternately to move or 'walk' across the length of the room and back again. It is best to start this exercise gradually, say once across the room, and work up to several times.

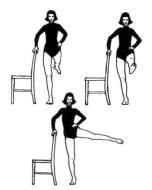

Exercise 9 Thighs often tend to get flabby and this exercise helps to rectify this and also firms up your hipline.

Place a dining room chair in the middle of the room and stand straight at the side of it. Grip the chair back with the nearest hand and rest the other hand lightly on your waist. Keeping your toe pointed and your knees straight, kick the outside leg forward and back as far as possible 10 times, then out sideways 10 times. Reverse your position and repeat with the other leg.

Exercise 10 This exercise trims and firms thighs, ankles and calves.

Stand straight with your legs and feet together, hands resting lightly on your hips. Breathe in deeply as you slowly rise on your toes, then breathe out as you lower your body to a deep knees bend. You can let your knees ease slightly apart as you bend, but your heels should not touch the floor. Breathe in as you rise slowly to your starting position. This exercise exerts strong pressure on your leg muscles, so start with just 1 or 2 bends and gradually work up to 8 times daily.

Exercise 11 This is an exercise for plump ankles, which you can do sitting down.

Sit down on a straight backed chair, cross your legs and with your big toe draw a large circle in the air, 10 times clockwise and then 10 times anti-clockwise. Do the same with the other foot.

Exercise 12 This is a good exercise for shoulder, back and breast muscles.

Stand up straight and place your hands lightly on your shoulders. Raise your elbows so that they are at right angles to your body. Now draw circles with your elbows as large as you can, so that you feel the pull on your muscles. Draw 10 circles, relax, and then repeat.

Slimming fashions

Nobody quite knows what to wear whilst losing weight on a diet. After all, there's no point in buying new clothes a few sizes smaller until you reach your target weight, is there?

Here are a few simple rules to follow.
Don't pick anything too tight or too loose. You musn't pick anything too drab in colour, nor a dress that's too pale. Palest beige, for example, would put hips on a snake!

Go for a simple, tailored style, and go gay on accessories. Chunky bracelets, elegant jewellery, bright hats, gay silk scarves, giant handbags— these are the kind of accessories that suit you.

Make up carefully, too, as this can take the eye of the viewer off your figure and on to your face while you are shedding weight.

Avoid minute or overlarge floral prints, also geometric designs which are large—they'd be more suitable hung up as curtains in the spare bedroom!

Try not to wear belts, they saw you in half visually. Non-waisted dresses are better every time than two-pieces and suits. If you must wear a two-piece, beware of a too-tight jacket or skirt. Trouser suits, if worn, must have long jackets—to cover the thigh tops.

Do, please, invest in a good foundation garment while you're on your diet. Plenty of time for carefree girdle-less days when you have reached to your ideal weight!

Choose dresses in a good fabric that hangs well and try to line all your dresses. Fabrics that hang well are bonded crêpes, silky looking ribbed Crimplene and Tricel jersey.

Always have a sleeve to cover the top of your arm, if the arm is large.

Make sure your stockings and tights fit well and give you sufficient support. Also, make sure the stocking is long enough and wide enough round the top.

If you're off on holiday and you need a swimsuit, have one made to measure with a built-in foundation.

To sum up. Loose, semi-fitted lines, stand-away collars, face-framing necklines, A-line dresses in dark or bright (not too pale) fabrics . . . all these suit you. Try walking about and try sitting down in a new dress when actually buying it, or being fitted, as freedom of movement is a release from feeling bulky, and whilst reducing weight, you must feel free to move.

Never try a dress on without wearing the right foundation underneath.

On a good slimming programme you will lose weight all over—even your feet will get slimmer. So be very careful and change your shoes the minute you feel them loose. Well-fitting shoes are essential for the support they give and whilst it is possible to alter the fit of a dress or skirt by unobtrusive darts here and there, you cannot do the same for a pair of shoes. New ones, which fit perfectly, are the only sensible answer.

Obviously you cannot buy a complete set of new clothes every time you go down one size, but please don't take the attitude that it doesn't matter how you look and keep wearing your dresses which are too large for you—at least not without altering them to fit. How you look does affect how you feel, and a little bit of alteration to some of your existing clothes will make you feel and look marvellous! Quite apart from anything else, this can be the spur that will keep you rigidly to your new eating habits.

Then, when you have reached your goal weight, how lovely to know that you can go out and gradually replenish your wardrobe, without feeling guilty about the dresses you have bought before time and no longer want to wear.

Index

CALORIE CHART

(Continued from front endpaper)

	Calories	Per
Margarine	226	1 oz.
Milk		
whole, silver or red top	380	1 Imp. pint
whole, gold top	490	1 Imp. pint
skimmed, fresh or reconstituted dried	200	1 Imp. pint
skimmed, dried (as powder)	93	1 oz.
buttermilk	110	½ Imp. pint
condensed (sweetened) milk	100	1 oz.
evaporated milk	50	1 fl. oz.
Oil		
corn oil	260	1 oz.
olive oil	264	1 oz.
Peanut butter	170	1 oz.
Suet	262	1 oz.
Yogurt		
natural, unsweetened	15	1 oz.
fruit, sweetened, average carton	160	carton

CEREALS AND STARCHES

	Calories	Per
All-Bran, cereal	88	1 oz.
Arrowroot	101	1 oz.
Barley, pearl		
raw	102	1 oz.
boiled	34	1 oz.
Bread		
white or brown	70	1 oz.
fresh breadcrumbs	70	1 oz.
Cornflakes, cereal	104	1 oz.
Cornflour (U.S. cornstarch)	100	1 oz.
Custard powder	100	1 oz.
Custard sauce (average)	27	1 oz.
Flour, plain (U.S. all-purpose) or self-raising	100	1 oz.
Macaroni		
raw	102	1 oz.
boiled	32	1 oz.
Noodles		
raw	102	1 oz.
boiled	32	1 oz.
Oatmeal, raw	115	1 oz.
Puff pastry, frozen	880	7½-oz. packet
	120	1 oz.
Ravioli, canned	527	15½-oz. can
	34	1 oz.
Rice		
raw	102	1 oz.
boiled	35	1 oz.
Ryvita, crispbread	98	1 oz.
Sago	101	1 oz.
Semolina	100	1 oz.
Spaghetti		
raw	104	1 oz.
boiled	36	1 oz.
Vitawheat, crispbread	120	1 oz.
Weetabix, cereal	100	1 oz.
Wheat germ	80	1 oz.

BISCUITS, CAKES AND PUDDINGS

	Calories	Per
Biscuits		
cream crackers	127	1 oz.
digestive (U.S. Graham crackers)	140	1 oz.
semi-sweet, mixed	125	1 oz.
sweet, mixed	160	1 oz.
water biscuits (U.S. crackers)	126	1 oz.

	Calories	Per
Cake		
sponge cake, average	87	1 oz.
jam Swiss roll (U.S. jelly roll), average	134	1 oz.
plain fruit cake, average	107	1 oz.
Doughnut, average	101	1 oz.
Gingerbread, average	108	1 oz.
Muffin (or crumpet), average	60	1 oz.
Pudding		
rice, average	42	1 oz.
suet, with raisins, average	100	1 oz.
Yorkshire pudding, average	63	1 oz.

SUGARY FOODS

	Calories	Per
Angelica, candied	90	1 oz.
Boiled sweets	93	1 oz.
Chocolate		
milk	167	1 oz.
plain (U.S. semi-sweet)	155	1 oz.
Fruit gums	49	1 oz.
Glacé (U.S. candied)		
cherries	67	1 oz.
apricots	50	1 oz.
Golden syrup (U.S. maple syrup)	84	1 oz.
Honey	82	1 oz.
Ice cream		
plain, vanilla	56	1 oz.
Cornish, vanilla	70	1 oz.
Jam	75	1 oz.
Jelly		
packet, sweetened	73	1 oz.
gelatine	70	1 oz.
Lemon curd	86	1 oz.
Marmalade	74	1 oz.
Mincemeat	37	1 oz.
Mixed peel	68	1 oz.
Stem ginger	85	1 oz.
Sugar, white or brown (granulated or castor)	112	1 oz.
Toffees	120	1 oz.
Treacle, black (U.S. molasses)	73	1 oz.

DRINKS

	Calories	Per
Alcoholic		
Beers		
Brown ale (U.S. dark beer), bottled	80	½ Imp. pint
Draught		
bitter	90	½ Imp. pint
mild	72	½ Imp. pint
Pale ale (U.S. light beer), bottled	92	½ Imp. pint
Stout		
bottled	100	½ Imp. pint
extra	111	½ Imp. pint
Strong ale	210	½ Imp. pint
Ciders		
dry	100	½ Imp. pint
sweet	120	½ Imp. pint
vintage	280	½ Imp. pint
Spirits		
brandy	63	⅙ gill
gin	55	⅙ gill
rum	75	⅙ gill
vodka	63	⅙ gill
whisky	63	⅙ gill